COMPETENCY-BASED EDUCATION
AND TRAINING IN PSYCHOLOGY

COMPETENCY-BASED EDUCATION AND TRAINING IN PSYCHOLOGY

A Primer

By

SCOTT W. SUMERALL, Ph.D.

Dwight D. Eisenhower Veterans Administration Medical Center

SHANE J. LOPEZ, Ph.D.

University of Kansas

MARY E. OEHLERT, Ph.D.

Director of Psychology Training
Dwight D. Eisenhower Veterans Administration Center

Charles C Thomas
PUBLISHER • LTD.
SPRINGFIELD • ILLINOIS • U.S.A.

Published and Distributed Throughout the World by

CHARLES C THOMAS • PUBLISHER, LTD.
2600 South First Street
Springfield, Illinois 62794-9265

©2000 by CHARLES C THOMAS • PUBLISHER, LTD.

ISBN 0-398-07041-5

Library of Congress Catalog Card Number: 99-057927

Printed in the United States of America
CR-R-3

Library of Congress Cataloging-in-Publication Data
Competency-based education and training in psychology : a
primer / edited by Scott W. Summerall, and Shane J. Lopez,
Mary E. Oehlert.
p. cm.
Includes bibliographical references and index.
ISBN 0-398-07041-5 (pbk.)
1. Psychology--Study and teaching (Graduate) 2. Psychology--
Study and teaching (Internship) I. Summerall, Scott. II. Lopez,
Shane J. III. Oehlert, Mary E.

BF77 .C59 2000
150'.71'1--dc21   99-057927

We would like to dedicate this book to our professors, persons
whom we respected and who opened up a range of possibilities,
and to those who have given us unending support.

to:
Ellen and Lauren-S.W.S.
to my wife, Allison Rose Lopez-S.J.L.
to John, Jane, Maichel, Beth, Bill, Paul, Pati, Luke,
and Dan–M.E.O.

FOREWORD

As educators and supervisors, competency is something we have often assumed in the past. If an individual passed knowledge-based tests or spent a certain amount of time with us on a rotation in an applied setting, we accepted they were competent to perform related tasks. However, students/interns may have been better served by a different mechanism to confirm they had learned what the course or experience was hoped to teach.

The call for competency-based education and training has been made. Many educators and direct-service supervisors, however, are unaware of how to go about implementing the new direction. The authors of *Competency-Based Education and Training in Psychology: A Primer* have elected to take on the task of bringing a variety of aspects of competency to the forefront. This is so that those who provide training in psychology can decide how to best utilize the concept of competency within their institution.

As this is a relatively new component of training in psychology, the literature on this topic is minimal. However, this text is able to offer information and ideas to consider before altering a program to adopt the competency-based model. The reader can expect this book to assist with (1) identifying areas of training where issues of competency should be applied, (2) reviewing how others in various disciplines have begun to address competency, (3) providing information on the available materials to assess competency, and (4) allowing for a discussion of the topic so that educators/supervisors can begin to implement this in the manner that best suits their setting and goals.

Developing strategies to train to, and assess, competency can be daunting. This book is quick, insightful, informative reading and can give direction when beginning the process. The authors are to be commended for helping the rest of us involved in psychology training chart unfamiliar territory.

Peggy J. Cantrell, Ph.D.
Director, Psychology Training
Veterans Administration Medical Center
Kansas City, Missouri

PREFACE

Training in psychology at the graduate and internship levels has been altered by accreditation standards. Increased attention is being given to the competence of the trainee. Is the student able to perform at a specified level? This perspective requires a modification in both teaching and assessment. This book is a primer, a text designed to expose professors and trainers of psychology students to data they may wish to consider during the course of their teaching. It presents some basic concepts of competency assessment and areas to evaluate.

We wish to thank all of the Dwight D. Eisenhower Veterans Administration Medical Center psychologists who have each taken an active role in developing a competency-based approach to our psychology training programs. In addition, we are grateful to all of our interns who, during the history of this training program, provided feedback and continue to give us insight into how to better provide supervision.

S.W.S.

S.J.L.

M.E.O.

CONTENTS

COMPETENCY-BASED EDUCATION AND TRAINING IN PSYCHOLOGY

Chapter 1

INTRODUCTION TO COMPETENCY-BASED EDUCATION AND TRAINING

Competency-based education and training (CBET) is not a new concept. In the field of preparing teachers for public schools, educators complained that student teachers were not being well-prepared for the functions of teaching. Some universities responded by including competencies within their curriculums. Most teacher education programs that developed such competencies did so in response to their state's teacher certification requirements (Mowder, 1979). The human resource management literature refers to the competencies required to perform various positions (Mitrani, Dalziel, & Fitt, 1992). However, competency-based training is relatively new in its wide application to psychology. The American Psychological Association (APA), in 1997, published new guidelines for professional psychology doctoral programs and internships. Emphasis was placed on ensuring the competence of the field's graduates, and thus holding training institutions and internships more closely accountable for the quality of professionals they produce.

The greatest difficulties in competency-based training are those of time and expense. Duties must be task analyzed, possibly requiring a substantial investment of time on the part of faculty and staff. Depending upon the techniques to be employed, the cost to develop assessment tools, training modules, etc. can be high. In addition, the time required to repeatedly assess students and provide frequent feedback can be considerable (Mowder, 1979).

3

Historically, students or interns could successfully complete a course or rotation and have demonstrated little that would indicate their competence in a given area. The student may have taken tests and demonstrated some basic knowledge or the intern may have seen a certain number of clients/patients. However, there was no obvious data that clearly confirmed competence in specific areas (e.g., rapport building). This is not to say that many institutions did not provide opportunities for students/interns to show competence. It is likely, though, that not all rotations or all courses required such. The APA guidelines changed this and directed the educators and trainers to assure that future psychologists had acquired information basic to psychology, had the requisite skills to practice, and had indicated such in a practical manner. The methods of accomplishing these tasks have been left up to the doctoral program and the internship site. The requirement to pursue competency, though, has left some psychologists unsure how to put the call for competency into action. *This text is a primer to provide suggestions and direction in training for and assessing professional competency of the persons who will soon enter the field of psychology and one day inherit it.*

WHAT IS COMPETENCY?

It is important to define competency at the outset. It refers not just to tasks, but to the understanding that the tasks are done effectively. A set of competencies are the behaviors necessary to perform one's job successfully, in addition to the knowledge requirements. Competency involves information as well as skill in applying that knowledge (Stratford, 1994), and has been defined in terms of three separate domains: what the individual brings to the job, what the individual does in the job, and what is achieved (Proctor, 1991). Thus, knowledge, performance, and outcome are essential features of competence.

Components of Competency

Stratford's (1994) review of competency revealed six components including being observable and measurable. Competencies need to be observable so that they can be measured. Competency that is unmeasurable prevents the educator from determining if the person has gained that particular skill.

Competencies should be containable and practical. In addition, there should not be so many competencies in any given subset that training becomes unwieldy. Woodruffe (1991), writing from a human resource management perspective, suggests an absolute maximum of 12 to 15 competencies within a subfield of an occupation. This would have to be altered for psychology as competence in biofeedback, for example, might require knowledge of musculature, psychopathology, pain management, and electronics, as well as the skill to engage in clinical interviews, apply electrodes, operate the equipment, and interpret findings. However, in keeping with the spirit of Woodruffe's suggestion, breaking skills down to extremely small units and assessing competency for each would be time-consuming and taxing for the educator and likely very frustrating for the student. It is recommended that competencies be broken down only to the point that it is practical and has a genuine impact on knowledge or skill.

Expertise is an important condition of setting competencies. Competencies should be derived from established persons in the field who are aware of change and can review competencies within a context of change. Without such, the competencies that might be developed may be stagnant and not adapt as the field progresses.

Flexibility is another of Stratford's (1994) components. The potential to be inflexible in how to complete a task suggests the formation of core competencies only. This would involve having basic knowledge and skills (e.g., research, assessment, relationship), but would not allow the individual to complete a specific task (psychotherapy: interpersonal or cognitive-behavioral; research: quantitative or qualitative) in the manner in which they and/or the client is best suited.

COMPETENCY-BASED MODELS

Fantuzzo (1984) outlined a model for competency-based training for psychologists. This involved three separate, but related, aspects: knowledge of fundamental psychological principles, mandatory skills, and legal and ethical restraints. Fantuzzo's proposal for competency began by requiring educators/trainers to identify the body of information necessary to effectively engage in a skill area. Once this has been accomplished, students are assessed to ensure they have adequately mastered the material. Table 1 demonstrates the full model which was denoted the MASTERY model.

Table 1
FANTUZZO'S (1984) MODEL OF COMPETENCY

Master Prerequisite Body of Knowledge
Assess Skill of Competency
Set Minimal Competency
Train to Competency
Evaluate Understanding of Relevant Legal and Ethical Principles
Review Skill Level
Yield to Continued Education

Skills central to practice must be determined and then a measurement instrument must be developed to objectively assess skills. Fantuzzo (1984) stated that a minimal standard must be set, below which one is not considered competent. Pretraining behavior is assessed initially followed by necessary education/training through video/audiotaping, oral feedback of specific skill deficiencies, information on common deficits and suggestions for remediation, and reassessment of skill. Once the person adequately demonstrates competence in a given area, they must show understanding of legal and ethical issues relevant to the practice of that skill. Fantuzzo recommended reviewing skill level even in experienced psychologists and, if necessary, taking refresher courses.

Reilly, Barclay, and Culbertson (1977) viewed assessment of competence as including knowledge, performance, and consequences (outcome). They described training programs which should address individualized instruction, instruction modules, variable time frames to assess rate of progress for each student, clinical settings and field work experience provided earlier in the education process, and an emphasis on exit rather than on entry criteria. An aspect of competency-based education that Reilly, et al. highlight is demonstrating the positive relationship between training and outcome of services provided to clients. Thus, institutions, including internship sites, are encouraged to routinely monitor the outcome of client services and modify training as necessary to ensure the best treatment is being provided.

Contracting

Teague (1983) developed a learning contract model for community psychology and specified learning objectives (e.g., develop skills as an evaluator and identify type of evaluation necessary, develop research design, etc.), tasks to meet learning objectives (e.g., choose a program to evaluate, do the evaluation using the following program evaluation methods, etc.), and resources to facilitate the learning objective (e.g., usage of materials from program evaluation course, weekly meetings with supervisor). Thus, students who come into a training setting wondering what they will do during a specified period of time can be assisted by supervisors who help them by refocusing on what skills they need to sharpen their professional development (Lykes & Hellstedt, 1987). A learning contract could be developed in practicum, internship, and postdoctoral settings as such allows all parties to know what is expected and, if there are deficits, what needs to be accomplished. Finally, individual meetings (at least once per semester) between the practicum instructor and onsite supervisor, once with the student present, and periodic phone calls assist with continuity of the competency model from classroom to clinic (Lykes & Hellstedt, 1987).

Concerns about Competency-Based Education and Training

Various fields have used or begun to use the concepts of competency-based training. These include music therapy (see Madsen & Alley, 1979), school psychology (see Kratochwill, 1982), nursing (see Schlomer, Anderson, & Shaw, 1997), medicine (see Hill, Stalley, Pennington, Besser, & McCarthy, 1997), and dentistry (see McCann, Babler, & Cohen, 1998). Competency-based education and training may be used to justify a field's existence, to ward off potential litigation, to keep in step with current trends, or to better define necessary skills graduates should be able to perform.

Conversely, Kratochwill (1982) stated there were "fundamental problems" (p. 977) in defining school psychology and its common elements or competencies. Some persons refer to CBET as reductionistic (Hyland, 1993) and something that ignores the intricacies of practice (Sambandan, 1995). Greenhalgh and Macfarlane (1997) stated that a competency-based model was a necessary but not sufficient process by which one could be trained to perform evidence-based practice. Schlomer, Anderson, and Shaw (1997) wrote that competency-based training may result in improved nursing skills. Hill et al. (1997) reported there was a "worldwide swing from the traditional to competency-based systems of medical education" (p. 136). Whatever the motivation may be and whatever the reservations some may have, the change to CBET appears to be widespread.

The application of CBET has been questioned as it may not be beneficial or desirable to reduce the role of a psychologist to small components (Mowder, 1982, cited in Kratochwill, 1982). The lessening of skills to subcomponents may result in more attention being given to easily measured behaviors (e.g., querying after a vague response on an intelligence test) and less to the more difficult to assess synthesis of skills (e.g., test interpretation, recommendation writing, giving information to families). However, CBET may ensure a relationship between instructional methods and goals (Kratochwill, 1982). Thus, if we know what our goal is, we can ensure that the individual gains the necessary information and skill to perform that task. Also, CBET relates an assessment of a student to a given objective. An important issue to consider is that psychology is not attempting to define a single set of skills that completely define a psychologist or dictate how students will be evaluated. Though we reference competencies defined by different groups and describe competency training models, there are many CBET methods and each school, internship site, or postdoctoral program can determine their own philosophy and approach to training (Kratochwill, 1982).

Evaluating Competencies

The type of assessment used to evaluate competence, or at least skill level, will vary depending upon the experience of the student. Different methods would be used to evaluate a novice as opposed to an expert. Chambers and Glassman (1997) provided a thorough and very informative discussion of CBET from the perspective of dental education. However, many of the concepts presented are applicable or modifiable to psychology. They utilize a developmental model to address issues of assessment. Psychologists in the training community (e.g., Hogan, 1964; Stoltenberg, 1981) have outlined therapists' development from student to professional.

Thus, in keeping with this perspective, evaluation should be viewed within a developmental framework.

The skills of novices are most appropriate for evaluation using tests (Chambers & Glassman, 1997). Novices require information to guide them and provision of information and assessment of comprehension is necessary.

More advanced graduate students, yet those who still are early in their educational careers or new to a particular type of material regardless of the academic level, can be assessed through simulation. This involves inspecting one's understanding and performance in situations that simulate some of the main features of practice. Methods may involve problem-based learning in groups or individually, close supervision in practica, essays, and reports. Those persons nearing competence to perform independently require evaluation of actual practice. Such techniques include case presentations and research studies. It is during this type of evaluation that ethics and professional behavior are best assessed (Chambers & Glassman, 1997). Assessment of actual practice, though, requires more subjective interpretation of performance. Dichotomous final decisions are made with this level of evaluation. The trainee passes or it is deemed that they have not demonstrated their ability to function autonomously. These are evaluations that should be conducted during advanced graduate standing and during internship. Exemplary products are cases that are well documented that may include reports, raw test results, psychotherapy notes, etc. and that demonstrate the person's particular skill in a, perhaps, difficult case. Test cases are unaided examples of work. They may occur under direct observation and the supervisor can assess the student's understanding of what is occurring and what should be done. Chambers and Glassman (1997) suggest the supervisor also can assess how the student integrates individual components of treatment (e.g., test results) with overall treatment (through case presentation and review of records) as well as practice management skills (through case selection, preparation, timeliness of reports and progress notes). The evaluation by portfolio is a combination of approaches. Faculty must take responsibility for identifying competencies. They are responsible for providing students the definitions of identified competencies and giving examples of how those competencies can be demonstrated accompanied by a timeline for completion. Students collect material demonstrating their competence and present it to the faculty.

Chambers and Glassman (1997) describe four categories that may facilitate judgments. "Qualified" are those persons who have achieved satisfactorily and are ready to move on in their professional development. "Becoming qualified" are persons who are progressing, but require additional experience to become competent to perform independently in a given area. "Not becoming qualified" are students who may require a modification of the manner in which the education is structured in order to succeed. "Unqualified" students are persons that reasonable accommodations cannot assist with moving forward. At first glance, the latter two categories are indistinguishable. Poor performance on tests in course work should not automatically result in dismissal. An evaluation is required to determine the nature of the difficulty. Is it due to poor study habits, insufficient academic background, etc.? Once a determination of the cause of the poor performance is made, remedial intervention should be attempted.

Chambers and Glassman (1997) include two final levels of skill, "Proficient" and "Expert." The former is a competent individual who is developing a professional identity and the latter has internalized their professionalism. Assessment of competence may occur periodically with these persons to ensure their skills are current and have not atrophied. This involves a self-analysis or a possible peer review. Specialty board certification tends to utilize exemplary products.

Basic Competency Model for Psychology

Competency, or the acquisition of competence, is a developmental process. As such, assessment of competency is also a developmental process. As with all developmental models, competency at one stage remains dependent on competency at preceding stages.

While it is assumed that the first stage of developing competency as a professional psychologist formally begins in graduate school with the acquisition of basic psychological knowledge, some would argue that the process actually begins as early as high school (Association of Psychology Postdoctoral and Internship Centers & American Psychological Association, 1997). Regardless of where one defines the beginning process, the core foundation is basic psychological knowledge. This basic knowledge is accumulated both through didactic experience and experiential endeavors such as practica, externships, internship, and postdoctoral training.

This book proposes a basic model of competency derived in large part from two sources: APA's guidelines and principles for accreditation (1996) and the 1989 National Council of Schools of Professional Psychology (NCSPP) San Antonio Conference summary (Peterson, McHolland, Bent, Davis-Russell, Edwall, Polite, Singer, & Stricker, 1991) which called for a competency-based model for training. Figure 1 (see page 15) presents a proposed model for competency training. The remainder of this chapter briefly addresses the definition of competencies at each stage whereas following chapters more fully address the definition and assessment of each of those competencies.

Basic Psychological Knowledge

The APA (1996) has established general criteria describing the basic body of knowledge in which professionals in psychology should be competent.

In achieving its objectives, the [graduate] program has and implements a clear and coherent curriculum plan that provides the means whereby all students can acquire and demonstrate substantial understanding of and competence in the following areas: (a)

The breadth of scientific psychology, its history of thought and development, its research methods, and its applications. To achieve this end, the students shall be exposed to the current body of knowledge in at least the following areas: Biological aspects of behavior; cognitive and affective aspects of behavior; social aspects of behavior; history and systems of psychology; psychological measurement; research methodology; and techniques of data analysis; (b) The scientific, methodological, and theoretical foundations of practice in the substantive area(s) of professional psychology in which the program has its training emphasis. To achieve this end, the students shall be exposed to the current body of knowledge in at least the following areas: individual differences in behavior; human development; dysfunctional behavior or psychopathology; and professional standards and ethics; (c) Diagnosing or defining problems through psychological assessment and measurement and formulating and implementing intervention strategies (including training in empirically supported procedures). To achieve this end, the students shall be exposed to the current body of knowledge in at least the following areas: theories and methods of assessment and diagnosis; effective intervention; consultation and supervision; and evaluating the efficacy of interventions; (d) Issues of cultural and individual diversity that are relevant to all of the above; and (e) Attitudes essential for life-long learning, scholarly inquiry, and professional problem-solving as psychologists in the context of an evolving body of scientific and professional knowledge. (APA, 1996, pp. 6-7)

This basic body of knowledge serves as the core on which future stages are built. Without the knowledge base, competency in practice cannot be achieved.

Building on a strong psychological knowledge base, the National Council of Schools and Programs in Professional Psychology (Peterson, et al. 1991) proposed the six competency areas which have been modified in the current model. The essence of the definitions, nevertheless, are consistent with these proposed by NCSPP.

Relationship is the capacity to develop and maintain a constructive working alliance with clients.

Assessment is an ongoing, interactive, and inclusive process that serves to describe, conceptualize, characterize, and predict relevant aspects of a client.

Intervention involves activities that promote, restore, sustain, or enhance positive functioning and a sense of well-being in clients through preventive, developmental, or remedial services.

Research involves a systematic mode of inquiry involving problem identification and the acquisition, organization, and interpretation of information pertaining to psychological phenomenon.

Education is the directed facilitation by the professional psychologist enhancing the growth of knowledge, skills, and attitudes in the learner whether that be student, client, or other professionals or family caregivers.

Management comprises those activities that direct, organize, or control the services that psychologists and other professionals offer or render to the public to include, but not limited to, supervision.

Advanced Clinical Skills are specialized in nature and require training beyond that expected of non-specialized clinician. Not every clinician will aspire or need advanced clinical training. Examples of areas of expertise requiring advanced clinical skills might be neuropsychology and forensic practice.

Ethics is the acquisition of knowledge and execution of problem-solving strategies in addressing conflicts related to moral values, ethics, and law.

Attitudes are cognitively acquired and behaviorally enacted in the understanding of such concepts as individual differences, cultural diversity, and professional development.

Fantuzzo's Model

The remaining chapters provide practical applications for competency-based training. While there are different models that one may use, in order to establish competency one must identify the core competency being assessed, develop a tool for assessing the core competency, and develop a plan to train to achieve that core competency. Fantuzzo (1984) developed the MASTERY model for CBET (see Table 2).

That particular model focuses on skill assessment. Thus, particularly in those stages where skill development is defined, the reader may notice an adaptation of components of Fantuzzo's model toward producing competency.

Table 2
COMPONENTS OF THE MASTERY MODEL

Master Prerequisite Body of Knowledge: Understand the psychological principles fundamental in the skill area.

Assess Skill Competency: Define the essential components of the skill in discrete observable behaviors.

Set Minimal Competency Standards: Identify the minimal skill necessary to assure effectiveness.

Train to Competency: Through a process of demonstration, evaluation, and feedback using the assessment tool developed above, the trainee is instructed (e.g. lecture, role model, practice exercises) and reassessed until minimal competency standards are achieved.

Evaluate Understanding of Relevant Legal and Ethical Principles: Objectively demonstrate understanding of ethics/legal ramifications.

Review Skill Level: Produce ongoing system for evaluation of skill level.

Yield to Continuing Education: Establish model for continuing to maintain skill level.

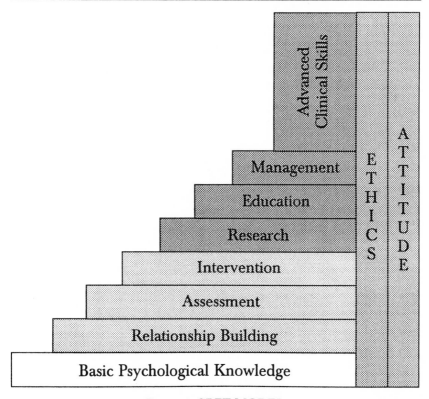

Figure 1. CBET MODEL

Chapter 2

ACQUIRING BASIC PSYCHOLOGICAL
KNOWLEDGE

A core body of psychological knowledge has developed over the decades and graduate and professional education in psychology is characterized by the dissemination of the common core (Fox & Barclay, 1989). Fifty years ago there was consensus about six knowledge areas (e.g., general psychology, psychodynamics of behavior, diagnostic methods, research methods, knowledge in related health disciplines, and psychotherapy). These have evolved into areas of fundamental knowledge, skills, and technique bases. Training programs and accrediting bodies have acknowledged this common knowledge base and have incorporated a core focus into training curriculum and accreditation guidelines. Within the proposed developmental competency model, a strong understanding of the core areas of psychology is the basic building block for professional competency in applied psychology. The APA, within the context of the accreditation guidelines for doctoral programs (1996), identified 11 areas as constituting the basic building blocks of psychological knowledge (see Table 3).

Table 3
CORE BODY OF PSYCHOLOGICAL KNOWLEDGE

Biological Aspects of Behavior
Cognitive and Affective Aspects of Behavior
Social Aspects of Behavior
History and Systems of Psychology
Psychological Measurement
Research Methodology
Techniques for Data Analysis
Individual Differences in Behavior
Human Development
Dysfunctional Behavior or Psychopathology
Professional Standards and Ethics

TRAINING AND ASSESSMENT OF COMPETENCY IN BASIC KNOWLEDGE AREAS

As the fundamental building block of competency in psychology, knowledge in the core areas is a prerequisite for building competencies and developing skills. Dissemination of information in these skill areas may start in secondary school and most certainly occurs in undergraduate psychology programs (APPIC & APA, 1997). However, graduate programs are required to expose their students to all of these areas. The APA accreditation guidelines (1996) are clear in their intent as they promote that "all students can acquire and demonstrate substantial understanding and competence in the aforementioned areas" (p. 6). Given the breadth of the knowledge base within each area, the task of promoting competency within each is a formidable one. Typically, doctoral programs entrust that students are exposed to necessary information in quality course offerings. In fact, the core curriculum of most doctoral programs is organized around these areas. These standard training practices have not been substantially modified since the call for competency-based training emerged, but the value of understanding basic psychological principles is emphasized within the developmental competency model and the MASTERY model of competency-based training. Mastery of the prerequisite knowledge that relates to clinical skills is essential. The components of objective competency-based training in the fundamental knowledge areas of psychology currently may be universally applied by graduate programs. Through didactic experiences, students are being exposed to fundamental psychological principles germane to clinical skills. However, there may be a weak link in training. Application and infusion of these fundamental principles in practicum and internship training may not occur in a systematic fashion. Thus, students may struggle to integrate basic knowledge and to understand the relationships between psychological principles and theory and therapy skills and techniques. This could stunt the development and usage of core competencies.

Training in Basic Knowledge Areas

To assist in the expansion of the core areas into practicum and internship training, one may consider a variety of options. Individual supervision sessions and case conferences may focus on the relevant ethical issues. APA guidelines, state laws, and court rulings may be discussed in seminar settings. Utilizing an understanding of human development can be useful in case conceptualization. When presenting a rationale for treatment, the trainee may provide a perspective as to how the chosen therapy relates to previous systems developed as therapeutic strategies. A greater emphasis may be placed on the biological bases of behavior in practicum placements and internships. This may entail discussing the impact of organ failure on cognition or how a damaged liver may interfere with the body's usage of psychotropic medication.

Obviously, there are many methods of incorporating the basic, core knowledge of psychology into applied experiences. This should not result in a reduction in the emphasis placed upon psychotherapy or assessment and related material (e.g., transference, boundary issues, etc.). However, it will help to provide a greater understanding of the client/patient and, therefore, allow improved services to be rendered.

Despite the traditional, yet unsystematic approach to competency-based training in this area, a multifaceted system of evaluating competencies has been implemented to insure mastery. However, comprehensive data on training and evaluation practices are not available. It is apparent that most psychology programs employ a two-pronged approach to evaluating competency in basic areas: (1) evaluation of course performance and (2) examination of general knowledge via comprehensive examinations or doctoral tasks. This system of evaluation is strengthened if the Examination for Professional Practice in Psychology (EPPP) is conceptualized as a third prong that addresses competency in the basic knowledge area. Building a fundamental knowledge in psychology facilitates the acquisition of higher order competencies. Accreditation guidelines dictate that training be provided in these areas and evaluation seems to guarantee the establishment of the basic building block of competency development.

How else does one go about assessing the core competencies? As noted previously, such is done primarily through graduate coursework, comprehensive examinations, and the licensure examination. By evaluating such knowledge during applied training also, one demonstrates its value and benefit to persons seeking treatment. Brief, objective measures conducted on internship may address ethics, biological bases of behavior, psychopathology, and multicultural issues. In addition, oral questioning during supervision and bed-rounds provide a basic understanding of knowledge. Case presentations and review of case notes give a more in-depth understanding as they may indicate how the person utilizes the core knowledge. It would be important to ascertain if the student/intern took into consideration potential medical and medication-related causes of poor performance (biological bases) on neuropsychological measures. Does the intern gain written approval before providing information about a client/patient to family members? Are they aware of prodromal signs of a specific disorder?

A single form to evaluate competency in the core areas would not be practical. This is because each site will have various emphases. Schizophrenia may be a common diagnosis in one setting, but rare in another. Therefore, competence in recognizing hallucinations may not be appropriate for both locations. Therefore, each site must develop its own set of competencies that it expects students/interns to demonstrate at completion of their training.

TRAINING IN CROSS-CULTURAL PRACTICE

With approximately one-fourth of the nation's citizens being of an ethnic/racial makeup other than Caucasian/European (Bernal & Castro, 1994), it is obvious why there is a need for an emphasis on cross-cultural training in graduate schools and at internship sites. Psychologists engage in a variety of tasks that can be affected by a person's cultural heritage. We may tend to use a somewhat macro view when attempting to determine the cultural applicability of psychological measures or in learning how cultural elements are demonstrated in therapy and focus on issues such as developing rapport or using proper norms.

Galanti (1991) provided a very informative discussion of various details of cultural differences. Competence with various cultures may include attention to issues such as hierarchical and egalitarian models of social structure. Some cultures may place greater emphasis on one's status as a function of age, sex, and occupation. The concept of time is another variable of importance to culture-specific psychological practice.

Some cultures accentuate one's family of origin versus the nuclear family. Even after marriage, there may be greater attention and importance placed upon the original family.

Extent and quality of eye contact may vary across cultures. To the Navajo, direct eye contact may be disrespectful. Furthermore, there may be a variation in the speed of response during communication. Some cultures find no discomfort in spending time to formulate a response. Thus, latency does not signify disinterest.

Usage of figures of speech can adversely affect communication between therapist and persons not fully aware of same. Galanti (1991) stated that referring to something as "silly" or "crazy" may be interpreted by non-native English speakers as the therapist believes it to be suggestive of being "mentally ill." Non-literal expressions such as having "cold feet" also are impediments to accurate communication. Even different cultures which utilize English may use words (particularly slang) differently resulting in misunderstandings.

Referring to someone by their first name may be considered appropriate among white middle-class Americans. However, if someone is not well acquainted with a person belonging to most other cultures (including European), utilizing a title (e.g., Mr., Ms.) is preferable. To do otherwise risks being considered impertinent.

Each of the above, and others, are components of cultures that require attention in order to provide competent services. Obviously, there is a knowledge element. This type of data can be provided in didactic course-work. As trainees work with members of various cultures during practica and internship, monitoring and educating/reeducating about these aspects are necessary to ensure the optimal level of treatment is being provided.

Defining and Assessing Competency in Cross-Cultural Practice

What is being assessed when measuring competency in multicultural psychological interventions? As the term multiculturalism is used to refer to such a variety of attributes of persons and as its operational definition may not be universally agreed upon, it is difficult for psychologists to focus on what they are expected to know and do (Helms & Richardson, 1997).

Attempts to define cross-cultural practice and multicultural competency have included Sodowsky, Taffe, Gutkin, and Wise (1994) who stated their view involved multicultural counseling skills (e.g., skills specific to a group, usage of nontraditional assessment methods, self-monitoring by the therapist, retention of minority clients), multicultural awareness (e.g., multicultural caseload, education/training/continuing education), and the multicultural counseling relationship (e.g., refraining from stereotyping, countertransference issues). Multicultural counseling knowledge (e.g., culturally relevant case conceptualization and treatment strategies, examination of cultural biases, self-monitoring, keeping current with the literature) completed their perspective.

Coleman (1997) broke down multicultural counseling competence into three areas. For individual intervention, the three areas included awareness (can the student recognize a cultural issue), knowledge (can the student describe a cultural etiology for a specific set of actions), and skills (can the student address a cultural concern within intervention).

Ridley, Espelage, and Rubinstein (1997) established a multicultural curriculum. Graduate courses should address issues of prejudice, racism, power, psychological assessment and diagnosis [to include confirmatory bias, fundamental attribution error, judgmental heuristics (Ridley, 1995)], counseling process and outcome goals, intervention tasks, multicultural counseling research, racial identity development, ethics specific to multicultural intervention, and norm development.

Sodowsky, Kuo-Jackson, and Loya (1997) provided clear guidance on areas to assess when conducting a family assessment from a multicultural perspective. Family composition (e.g., members, is there a hierarchy, living arrangements, decision-making style), primary caregivers, perception by family of the problem (e.g., understanding of fate, willingness to share with outsiders, to what does the family assign the cause of the problem), family's perception of health and healing and intervention, language, interaction styles (e.g., emotion, is communication direct or indirect, loud or quiet, etc.). As appropriate, each of these should be addressed by the trainee when engaging in cross cultural intervention. The supervisor may wish to review these and other areas to determine whether the student is considering relevant variables.

A component of the competency checklist used by Ponterotto (1997) addressed evaluating students' cross-cultural competency. Yearly and end-of-program evaluations could include a determination of their sensitivity to, knowledge, and skill in multicultural issues. Knowledge of multicultural intervention can also be assessed on comprehensive examinations.

Some schools and training sites may want to utilize a collection of materials to document competence (Coleman, 1997). This approach can include notation of the cultural groups served, written information pertaining to variables affecting intervention (e.g., communication styles, family issues, etc.), and evidence of their skill in applying their awareness and knowledge (e.g., videotapes, transcripts).

Various instruments have been developed to assess competency related to multicultural psychological practice. The supervisor may wish to select from the Cross-Cultural Counseling Inventory-Revised (LaFramboise, Coleman, & Hernandez, 1991), Multicultural Counseling Awareness Scale-Form B: Revised Self-Assessment (Ponterotto, Sanchez, & Magids, 1991), Multicultural Awareness-Knowledge-and-Skills Survey (D'Andrea, Daniels, & Heck, 1991), and the Multicultural Counseling Inventory (Sodowsky, Taffe, Gutkin, & Wise, 1994). The Cultural Sensitivity Self-Report (Lopez, 1996; see Appendix A) can be used to assess cultural sensitivity, the preresponse behavior that is related to cross-cultural counseling competency (Ridley, Mendoza, Kanitz, Angermeier, & Zenk, 1994).

Ensuring that multicultural information and practice is taught and then assessing students' understanding and utilization of the material are necessary conditions of modern psychological training. Competence to practice with persons from varied cultural backgrounds is currently and will continue to become increasingly important.

Chapter 3

TRAINING IN RELATIONSHIP BUILDING

BASIC KNOWLEDGE IN RELATIONSHIP BUILDING

Relationship competency is "the capacity to develop and maintain a constructive working alliance with clients," (Peterson, et al., 1991, p. 77). Polite and Bourg (1991) suggested that the "relationship competency is the foundation and prerequisite for all other competencies in professional psychology...[it is] the basic ability to establish, understand, and maintain authentic and appropriate relationship," (p. 83). In fact, C. H. Patterson (1974) suggested "that psychotherapy is a relationship. It is assumed that providing a facilitative or therapeutic relationship is the necessary and sufficient condition for helping those persons who are failing to develop or progress toward self-actualizing behavior," (p. 49). Research on common factors of psychotherapy (Frank, 1961) supported this statement.

What components then are necessary to build relationships? What basic knowledge is necessary prior to beginning relationship building? Patterson (1974) conceptualized relationship building in response dimensions, action dimensions and implementation of dimensions. From another perspective, Othmer and Othmer (1994) conceptualized stages in relationship building including the initial stages of rapport building and strategies or techniques for getting information.

25

Patterson's Model

Response dimension refers to the therapist's basic response to the client. Carl Rogers (1957) suggested three core conditions or responses necessary on the part of the therapist essential to establishing therapeutic relationships: empathy, unconditional positive regard (or respect) and congruence (or genuineness). Truax and Carkuff (1964) offered concreteness, or the ability to use specific and concrete terminology rather than vague and abstract terminology, as a fourth condition leading to differentiation of feelings and experiences.

Empathy has been described as "ability to put one's self in another's boots [moccassins]" or ability to "get under one's skin and feel as they do." It is understanding not the details of a person's life but how they think and how they feel. Unconditional positive regard has also been referred to as respect.

Unconditional suggests that the positive regard is not conditional upon the client/patient behavior. The therapist responds with respect regardless of the behavior, the therapist exudes warmth and caring for the personal worth of the individual.

Congruence, also known as genuineness, encourages the therapist to be themselves; open, honest, sincere. The therapist does not think one thing and say another, rather a therapeutic relationship requires the integration of the therapist with the client/patient. "Genuineness does not require that the therapist always express all his feelings; it only requires that whatever he does express is real and genuine and not incongruent." (Patterson, 1974, p.64).

Concreteness, as defined by Truax and Carkhuff (1964), is the opposite of generalization. Particularly early in the therapeutic process, concreteness encourages the pursuit of specific details to ensure the accuracy of understanding by both parties. "Concreteness serves three important functions: (a) it keeps the therapist's response close to the client's feelings and experiences; (b) it fosters accurateness of understanding in the therapist, allowing for early client corrections of mis-understanding; and (c) it encourages the client to attend to specific problem areas" (Patterson, 1974, p. 68).

Othmer and Othmer's Model

Othmer and Othmer (1994) provided six steps for building rapport. The initial stage for relationship building is establishing rapport. The first step is to put the patient, and oneself, as the therapist, at ease. Very basically, this requires recognition and response to signs of "dis-ease." Signs may be gleaned verbally (either content or voice inflection), emotionally, behaviorally (e.g. psychomotor agitation), or territorially (e.g. where patient sits). Once the signs are recognized they must be responded to in an assuring manner.

The second step is detecting suffering and showing compassion. Determining how a patient is suffering may be as easy as asking the patient to tell you what is bothering them. The recommended response to finding the suffering is empathy.

The third step is assessing the client/patient's insight and to become an ally. They suggest that if you "misjudge the patient's level of insight, rapport will deteriorate rapidly" (p. 24). There are three levels of insight: (1) full insight reflects an understanding by the patient that their symptoms are a result of a disorder; (2) partial insight might best be characterized by the patient who recognizes that they are having difficulties but places blame on external circumstance; and (3) no insight reflects a lack of understanding regarding their difficulties (e.g. delusional disorder) and is often characterized by the individual who is "brought" to therapy by family or friend. Allying oneself requires that you focus on the healthy side of the patient and set treatment goals that will support their level of insight.

The fourth step (show expertise) and the fifth step (establish leadership) are intertwined. To show expertise the therapist must first help the patient put the illness into perspective (e.g. do you know of someone else who has suffered this disorder, what do you understand about the disorder, etc.). Once the therapist understands the client's perspective on the disorder process, the therapist can reveal their knowledge and potentially demystify the suffering. Then the therapist must be ready to deal with doubts the client has about getting better and provide or instill hope. Leadership is established when one is able to motivate the client to change. At the point that the client actively accepts and participates or "buys into" the treatment regimen, one is assured of leadership. Leadership is not forced upon the client, but rather grows out of successfully achieving the previous steps.

The final step is balancing the roles. The therapist must balance the role of empathic listener, expert, and leader. The client's roles will also change throughout the therapeutic process. The client may assume a number of roles (e.g., the sufferer, the very important person, the carrier of an illness, etc.). Rapport happens when the therapist balances their role with the role that the patient is playing.

Once rapport is established, Othmer and Othmer (1994) suggested the necessity of some basic strategies for maintaining the relationship and gathering information. They divide these strategies according to three patient types. "A patient generally communicates his problems in one of three ways: (1) by pouring it all out (complaints); (2) by revealing some problems but concealing the embarrassing items (resistance); or (3) by obfuscating the most embarrassing part to you, and even to himself (defenses)" (p. 44).

Othmer and Othmer suggested that each of these types respond best to different relationship-maintaining strategies. For instance, strategies for dealing with complainers include opening techniques, clarification techniques, and steering techniques.

Resistors, on the other hand, show some reluctance to speak about certain areas of their lives. A key to getting resistors to open up, then, is acceptance or as described earlier, unconditional positive regard. Building on the core of providing acceptance, other techniques that can be used include confrontation (focusing the client's attention on the resistance), shifting (approaching a problem from another direction), exaggeration (puts symptom in perspective by comparing to an exaggerated response), or in some cases even enticing the client to brag about their symptoms.

Finally, for the defensive client, the therapist must first have knowledge of the basic defenses and defense mechanisms utilized by clients. Defense mechanisms distort the patient's perceptions of themselves and/or their environment. Techniques offered by Othmer and Othmer (1994) for handling defense mechanisms include bypassing (e.g. let sleeping dogs lie), distraction, confrontation (drawing a patient's attention to a particular behavior), and interpretation (e.g. interpreting the reason for the defense back to the client.)

In summary, competence in relationship building requires skills necessary to build and maintain working therapeutic alliances. Skills used for building relationships include expressing empathy, unconditional positive regard, congruence, and concreteness along with the ability to build rapport with the client. Basic strategies or techniques for gathering information are also required in order to provide growth and thus maintain the therapeutic relationship.

In keeping with the spirit of competency training, the need to evaluate the learner must occur even with an ambiguous concept such as relationship building. The next section applies components of Fantuzzo's (1984) MASTERY model to the assessment of relationship competence.

APPLICATION OF THE MASTERY MODEL

Master Prerequisite Body of Knowledge

As with any area of competence, the scope of knowledge, or the ultimate goals of the training, need to be clearly specified. It is proposed that basic competence in relationship building could include, but not necessarily be limited to, the following:

1. Understand and demonstrate Carl Roger's (1957) three core elements of relationship building: empathy, unconditional positive regard, congruence (see Appendices B, C, & D).
2. Understand and demonstrate Carkhuff and Truax (1964) core element of concreteness (see Appendix E).
3. Understand and demonstrate rapport building strategies (see Appendix F).
4. Understand and demonstrate strategies for gathering information on the client/patient presentation (see Appendix G).

Many may feel that the area of cultural competence is best placed within the relationship competency area. Although the authors support this conceptualization, as it is such a basic requirement to conducting psychological treatment, it is positioned within the Fundamental Knowledge Base section of this text. Therefore, the reader should consult Chapter 2 for this area of knowledge and skill within the field.

Assessment of Skill Competency

Once the scope of competence is defined, the next step is to objectively assess whether or not competence has been achieved. There are a variety of ways to assess competency in any area. While "examinations" may be the best way to assess knowledge base, it is not necessarily the most appropriate means of assessing the application of knowledge. Using the internship year as the training period, it is assumed that mastery of basic knowledge should be present on entry into the internship. It is further assumed that demonstration or application of the knowledge should be present prior to completion of the internship.

Training to competency at the knowledge level would include providing literature, training seminars as needed, and test/retest opportunities. Methods for training to competency at the skill level could include reviewing audio/videotapes of the trainee with clients. Supervisors could provide ongoing assessment of tapes until competency is routinely achieved.

Example: Internship Year–Completion

1. Demonstrate knowledge and entry level ability to apply Carl Roger's (1957) core elements to relationship building.
2. Demonstrate knowledge and entry level ability to apply Carkhuff and Truax (1964) principle of concreteness.
3. Demonstrate knowledge and entry level ability to apply rapport–building strategies.
4. Demonstrate knowledge and ability to use strategies for gathering additional information.

Set Minimal Competency Standards

Minimal standards should be set for knowledge and skills. Carkhuff and Truax developed a five level system for evaluating empathy, genuineness, respect, and concreteness (Patterson, 1974). For example, level 1 for evaluating respect suggests "the verbal and behavioral expressions of the first person communicate a clear lack of respect (or negative regard) for the second person" (p. 59) whereas the facilitator in level 5 "communicates the very deepest respect for the second person's worth as a person and his potentials as a free individual" (p. 60). Skill level should be at level 3. One might also set minimum standards for rapport-building skills and identifying and demonstrating strategies for gathering information.

Once again, a written exam is probably the best way to assure basic knowledge. It is assumed having knowledge of the core requirements precedes ability to demonstrate skill in using them. Minimal competency standards for application of skills (Empathy, Unconditional positive regard, Congruence, and Concreteness) is level three as assessed by Carkhuff and Truax as cited by Patterson (1974). Minimal competency standards for rapport building is 50 percent of all applicable indicators. On entry into a program, interns might videotape a role play with each other in which one intern is the client and another is the therapist. They could be given a vignette to act out with instructions that the "therapist" is to demonstrate their basic relationship-building skills. They would then be assessed using the scales described earlier.

Training for Competency

Audiotaping and videotaping sessions with one-on-one supervision using the scales mentioned previously may assist with training students who require further refinement of skill level. Trainees may rate their own work and then compare their ratings with the ratings of supervisors. Discrepancy between trainee and supervisee ratings can be a source of discussion with reviewing video/audiotapes together. Also, a second supervisor can independently rate the trainees' performance. Case presentations where the intern shows clips from several sessions with the client/patient can provide evidence of the trainee to maintain the relationship across time.

Chapter 4

TRAINING IN ASSESSMENT

The "...best hope for clinical psychology to overcome legal and economic challenges lies in the profession's ability to fortify itself with more objective competency-based training and evaluation procedures" (p. 31). This may sound like the current sentiment in the field, but it is actually a view espoused by the American Psychological Association Task Force on the Evaluation of Education, Training, and Service in Psychology (APA, 1983) and cited by Moon, Fantuzzo, and Gorsuch (1986). Despite the need for competency-based assessment training, the challenge of "doing more with less" is accentuated by cuts in training funds and by an increased demand for graduate training in psychology.

Though training faculty in graduate, internship, and postdoctoral programs may attempt to provide competency-based training in various areas of practice, training to competence in assessment seems to challenge trainers at all levels. In fact, the lack of assessment skills has been identified as the primary deficit of internship applicants (Garfield & Kurtz, 1973; Lopez, Oehlert, & Moberly, 1996). This "lack" of competency may be attributable to the difficulty doctoral programs have in identifying and implementing time-effective and cost-efficient training models in the clinical curriculum. Doctoral students' assessment skill deficits then become the concern of internships and postdoctoral training programs.

Competency-based training in assessment is particularly difficult because the total training time needed to obtain competency exceeds that offered within a three or four credit course. Assessment is an extremely complex ongoing, interactive, and inclusive process that serves to describe, conceptualize, characterize, and predict relevant aspects of a client. Thus, training to competence in the assessment area is a challenge that has been highlighted by several authors (e.g., DeCato, 1992; Fantuzzo, Sisemore, & Spradlin, 1983). This reality is suggested by the adage which reveals the complexity of psychological testing, "you cannot interpret what you cannot score and you cannot score what you cannot administer." Thus, it would seem that competency-based training in the assessment area naturally would begin with the testing aspects of the assessment process. That is, the rudimentary skills of administering and scoring the more popular measures should be mastered before interpretation, integration of data, and diagnosing difficult cases are addressed.

TRAINING TO COMPETENCE: MASTERY AND OTHER FORMS OF ACTUALIZING THE IDEAL

An assessment competency mandate has been promulgated by the recent APA Ethical Principles of Psychologists and Code of Conduct (APA, 1992), by the Standards for Educational and Psychological Testing which are currently being revised, and by position statements made by various professional organizations. Despite this call, few objective competency-based training and evaluation procedures have been developed. In fact, a review of the literature presents only one model for assessment training and a few attempts at actualizing the ideal of competency-based training.

The MASTERY Model

The first well-disseminated objective competency-based training model was developed and validated by John Fantuzzo. The MASTERY model "transmits training mandates into a viable training paradigm: (1) evaluates competence in terms of discrete behaviors, (2) assesses performance as close to criterion as possible; and (3) provides measurement conditions that closely approximate actual clinical situations" (Fantuzzo & Moon, 1984, p. 1055). The training model (outlined in the "Rediscovering Mastery: An Integrated Approach" section of this chapter) requires students study an administration and scoring manual for 1-2 hours prior to their first administration. Then the measure is administered to a volunteer (this session is observed by a trainer and is followed by feedback of their administration; this may be facilitated by discussing the results of an administration and scoring criteria checklist for that measure). Then students attend a one-hour lecture which focuses on common administration pitfalls, and ethical and legal issues related to assessment. After the lecture, students view a videotape demonstrating accurate administration procedures and complete their second administration with a volunteer.

The model has been applied to the teaching of Wechsler Adult Intelligence Scale-Revised (Fantuzzo & Moon, 1984; Moon, Fantuzzo, & Gorsuch, 1986) and the Wechsler Intelligence Scale for Children-Revised (Fantuzzo, Sisemore, & Spradlin, 1983). An automated version of the MASTERY model (i.e., videotapes and administration examples guide trainees through the learning experience) was also identified as an effective training procedure (Blakely, Fantuzzo, & Moon, 1985). Empirical investigation into this model suggests that it "provides a system for objectively ensuring and assessing knowledge pertaining to a specific skill, level of skill proficiency, and an understanding of issues," (Blakely, Fantuzzo, & Moon, 1985. p. 641).

The Manualized Approach

The MASTERY model is a comprehensive system of training. Other trainers have presented approaches that respond to the competency mandate by developing competency-based teaching materials, or a teaching/training manual.

The manualized approach, although not previously referred to as such in the literature, has been used by DeCato (1992) and the team at Rorschach Workshops. The approaches stem from trial and error in the classroom and workshop. "Developing a manual of practice materials with classified criteria including access to immediate scoring feedback seemed a logical way to approach the problem..." (DeCato, 1992, p. 61). Thus, one might develop training manuals that include protocols from patients which reveal many of the difficult aspects of administration and scoring. These protocols should be reviewed by several psychologists with years of experience with the measure to ensure that appropriate administration and scoring procedures have been applied. Then, protocols should be compiled into a manual that includes feedback sheets, competency checklists, and interpretive guidelines. Students could be exposed to this manualized approach in a classroom setting, workshop format, or independent study.

Identifying Problem Areas in Administration and Scoring

Remember, one cannot interpret what cannot be scored, and one cannot score what one cannot administer. Thus, researchers have examined the evidence suggesting that students and practitioners do err when administering and scoring standardized measures. This body of literature has been generated by one camp comprised of Slate and colleagues. Research has focused specifically on errors made when working with the Wechsler Scales and on the effects of practice administration on reducing errors. Common errors in Wechsler Scale administration are highlighted in Table 4. Many of these errors are easily avoidable.

Table 4
COMMON ADMINISTRATION AND SCORING ERRORS ON THE
WECHSLER SCALES (PRESENTED IN ORDER OF FREQUENCY OF
OCCURRENCE)

WPPSI-R Errors (Whitten, Slate, Jones, Shine, & Raggio, 1994)
Failure to record examinee responses, circle scores, or record times
Assigned too many points to examinee response
Failure to obtain a correct ceiling
Failure to question when required by a test manual
Assigned too few points to examinee response
Incorrect point value assigned for Performance items
Failure to obtain a correct basal
Questioned when not appropriate

WISC-R Errors (Slate & Jones, 1990)
Failure to record examinee responses, circle scores, or record times
Assigned too many or too few points to examinee response
Questioned when not appropriate (typically failed to ask questions)
Failure to obtain correct basal or ceiling
Incorrect raw score total for subtests
Incorrect calculation of chronological age
Incorrect point value assigned for Performance items

WAIS-R Errors (Slate, Jones, Murray, & Coutler, 1993)
Failure to record examinee responses, circle scores, or record times
Failure to question when required by a test manual
Assigned too many points to examinee response
Questioned when not appropriate
Failure to obtain a correct ceiling
Assigned too few points to an examinee response
Incorrect raw score total for subtests
Incorrect calculation of chronological age
Incorrect conversion of Scale scores to IQs
Incorrect total of Verbal and Performance Scores

Though not empirically substantiated, it would seem that these findings may generalize to the recent revisions of the WISC and the WAIS. Little data about the frequency of administration and scoring errors for other measures are available. However, a list of common errors could be generated after observing a student's first administration of a measure.

Given information about common errors, trainers could offer a piece of the MASTERY approach by lecturing on common pitfalls encountered when working with particular measures. This lecture, along with immediate direct feedback after a student's first administration of a measure, could be the groundwork for increasing competency in assessment. Trainers could also facilitate a discussion of scoring rules and practice on difficult-to-score items. This would help reduce examiner error. The efforts at increasing accuracy would be made so that "practice does not make perfect errors."

The statement "practice makes perfect errors" alludes to research that suggests examiners often practice errors and experience "negative transfer" of administration errors from one test to another (Slate, Jones, & Murray, 1991). These findings highlight the need for discussion and careful application of complicated scoring rules, and of providing feedback immediately after initial administration techniques.

Rediscovering MASTERY: An Integrated Approach

This approach was developed in the early 1980s and the extent to which it is applied is unclear. The focus of the model, as applied to assessment, is on training students to master the rudimentary skills in assessment, administration and scoring. Competency-based training in assessment cannot be limited to competency-based training in psychological testing. Interpretation, diagnostic accuracy, report writing, the provision of feedback need to be addressed in competency-based training framework for assessment. Thus, an expanded MASTERY model is proposed.

MASTERY: An Integrated Approach Incorporates the MASTERY Model and the Manualized Approach

Table 5 provides a snapshot of what this revised model involves. For the purpose of demonstrating how the model can be applied, a process for MASTERY training for administration and scoring for the WAIS-III, Table 6 presents the stages of the model and the corresponding WAIS-III training techniques.

Table 5
MASTERY: AN INTEGRATED APPROACH

Training to competency in administration and scoring (Fantuzzo model)
Training to competency in interpretation (Manualized approach)
Training to competency in report writing (Manualized approach)
Training to competency in providing feedback (Manualized approach and video review)
Training to competency in diagnosing

Table 6
COMPONENTS OF THE MASTERY MODEL AND CORRESPONDING
WAIS-III TRAINING STEPS

Master Prerequisite Body of Knowledge
Student completes coursework in measurement, assessment, and intelligence theory.
Student views The Psychological Corporation videos that describe the WAIS-III.
Student reviews the WAIS-III manual for at least two hours and becomes familiar with the testing materials.

Assess Skill Competency
Student administers the entire WAIS-III to a non-patient volunteer while being observed by a trainer who is assessing skill competency with the Administrative Checklist for the WAIS-III (Sattler & Ryan, 1999).
Student completes scoring, derives summary scores, and converts scales to IQ.
Trainer reviews accuracy of administration and scoring.
Trainer provides immediate feedback to student.

Set Minimal Competency Standard
Trainer sets a clear competency standard such as 90 to 95% administration and scoring accuracy as determined by review of the WAIS-III Administrative Checklist.

Train to Competency
Trainer presents a lecture on the common errors made in the administration and scoring of the WAIS-III.
Student views a video highlighting accurate administration and scoring procedures.
Student completes additional trainer-evaluated or peer-evaluated WAIS-III administrations (3 or more) until the competency standard is met.

Evaluate Understanding of Relevant Ethical and Legal Principles

Trainer presents a lecture on the ethical and legal issues related to intelligence testing. Student obtains a passing grade on a quiz over ethical and legal principles.

Review Skill Level

Student's WAIS-III administration and scoring skills are reevaluated periodically, over the course of the quarter or semester or over the internship or postdoctoral year(s).

Yield to Continuing Education

Trainers provide students with continuing education information and opportunities.

Upon achieving competency in the administration and scoring of a measure, the focus of training shifts to interpretation and report writing. A manual that includes five or more protocols reflective of commonly encountered, yet complex cases can facilitate a training process that will allow students to be trained to a criterion.

Interpretation of these protocols should follow a series of lectures focusing on test interpretation. Then, the trainer could demonstrate the interpretive process through examination of the first protocol in the manual. The student could then attempt a profile interpretation and complete an interpretive checklist.

The checklist should reflect the major interpretive components that the student should have examined. Responses to the "yes/no" format yields basic interpretive accuracy when compared to the criterion measure. Immediate feedback to the student's attempt at interpretation should be provided and a brief lecture designed to highlight the difficult aspects of this particular case should be given by the trainer. The remaining protocols should be interpreted and reviewed. A predetermined minimal competency standard, assessed by the interpretive checklist, could be established as the competency-based training goals.

Objective competency-based training in report writing and the provision of feedback may be a more difficult ideal to actualize as criterion is difficult to establish. However, lectures and report examples set expectations for what elements should be included. Report checklists could be developed to assess competency and feedback should be offered immediately after the completion of each report. A criterion report should be added to the manual after the student has completed the report and has received feedback. This report should be reviewed with the student to highlight aspects of a report that accurately and effectively communicate the test interpretation. Report writing experiences should be provided to the student until a competency standard is met.

Training students to provide feedback to patients could be facilitated via lecturing on the feedback process and viewing a feedback session based on the data and clinical situation described in the first case in the manual. Key elements in the feedback process could be demonstrated and reviewed. Students would then facilitate a videotaped role-play of a feedback session for the remaining cases. After each session, the tape should be reviewed by the trainer and student. Establishing criteria for competent feedback would be determined by the trainer as the training literature does not specify aspects of competent feedback provision.

Training in diagnosing is a complex endeavor that involves the examination of student bias, use of heuristics, knowledge of diagnostics categories and pathology, and clinical judgment and decision-making. Competency-based training in the diagnostic competence of assessment has not been widely addressed in psychology literature. Though diagnostic accuracy is a training goal that trainers hope all students attain, the process of providing competency-based training in this area is not well-established. Thus, trainers who take on the task of developing a training component that addresses diagnostic accuracy should attempt to address the plethora of complex issues related to psychodiagnostics.

Summary

This sketch of MASTERY: An Integrated Approach to competency-based training in assessment offers some of the building blocks that could be incorporated into a training program. Though it extends a previously formulated model for training, it does not address all issues involved in training students to be competent practitioners in the assessment area. It is offered as a guide to those who are attempting to incorporate objective training that evaluates competence in terms of discrete behaviors and assesses performance as close to the criterion as possible (Fantuzzo & Moon, 1984).

Competency-Based Training Tools

This chapter describes approaches to actualizing the ideal of providing competency-based assessment training. The feasibility of applying such approaches varies with training programs. However, some of the competency-based training tools could be used in any setting to promote competency. For example: Criteria for Competent WAIS-R Administration (Fantuzzo & Moon, 1984), Administrative Checklist for the WAIS-III (Sattler & Ryan, 1999), Criteria for Competent WISC-R Administration (Fantuzzo, Sisemore, & Spradlin, 1983), Administrative Checklist for WMS-III (Ryan, Weaver, & Lopez, 1999).

Chapter 5

TRAINING IN INTERVENTIONS

Intervention competency is said to "involve activities that promote, restore, sustain, or enhance positive functioning and a sense of well-being in clients through preventive, developmental, or remedial services," (Peterson, et al., 1991, p. 78). This definition, no doubt purposefully broad, alludes to the wide range of "therapies" that are employed by psychologists as they intervene with clients presenting with a vast array of problems. How then does one begin to assess competency in interventions? How does one even begin to categorize interventions? It is understood that intervention may involve pain management, cognitive rehabilitation, industrial/organizational techniques with a corporation, and many others. However, for the purposes of serving as an example, this chapter will limit intervention to psychotherapeutic activities.

On a very simple level, interventions might be organized by components such as the number of clients included in the intervention (individual, couples, family, group) or the age of the client (infant, child, adolescent, adult, geriatric adult). While seemingly simple classifications, these components or characteristics of interventions are of sufficient importance to warrant many licensing boards to seek verification that one is competent to practice within these parameters.

At another level, interventions might be classified in terms of complexity and/or acuteness or chronicity of the patient's presenting problem. In individual therapy, the lowest level of complexity might be the patient with a single, focal, acute diagnosis. This level would be for patients with an Axis I diagnosis. Perhaps at the next level of complexity would be patients with dual diagnosis, cognitive impairment, social or familial impairment or complex psychiatric and/or behavioral deficits. At the most complex level patients would be patients with chronic level psychosis and/or personality disorders.

With group therapy, the lowest complexity level might be co-facilitation with a senior level psychologist. Middle-level complexity might include sole leadership of a psychoeducational or highly structured group with high functioning patients. Finally, at the most complex level, the therapist would demonstrate ability to lead a therapy process group with a blend of diverse patients.

Beyond the mode of intervention, the characteristics of clientele, and/or the complexity of intervention, the question of competency of specific types of interventions still needs to be addressed. How does one decide with which intervention(s) a beginning level psychologist should be competent? What is necessary to demonstrate competence with a given specific intervention such as cognitive, behavioral, transtheoretical, or one of over 300 different types of therapy?

Beck (1976) offers some suggestions for addressing the plethora of psychotherapies. First, he draws a distinction "between a system of psychotherapy and a simple cluster of techniques," (p. 306) the latter having relatively no importance in the competency issues. He promotes the concept of the "well-developed system of psychotherapy," (p. 306). To qualify as a system, two primary components are mandatory. First, there must be a comprehensive theory (or model) of psychopathology. Second, there must be a detailed description of therapeutic techniques related to the model. Although he does not address competency in interventions, one might reasonably conclude that in order to be competent in any well-developed system of psychotherapy, one must first understand and be able to clearly articulate the theory of psychopathology out of which the techniques grow. Next, one must understand and be able to articulate the relationship between the techniques and the theory. Finally, one needs to be able to demonstrate an ability to implement the techniques given a clear knowledge of the theory supporting the therapy.

Beck (1976) outlined five criteria or standards for evaluating theories of psychopathology:

1. The theory should satisfy the requirements of any good scientific theory, namely, that it explains the phenomenon within its domain with minimal complexity.
2. The theory of psychopathology should be closely related to its allied psychotherapy so that is obvious how the psychotherapeutic principles are logically derived from the theory.
3. The theory should provide the basis for understanding why its derived psychotherapeutic techniques are effective. The rationale and mode of operation of the therapy should be implicit in the theory.
4. The theory should be elastic enough to allow for development of new techniques without being so loose or complex that it obligingly dispenses a justification for any procedure a therapist might feel inspired to improvise.
5. An important challenge to a scientific model is the degree to which it is based on verified evidence. (pp. 307-308)

It is recommended that each educational and training institution determine what therapies it believes it can adequately teach and in which it can provide supervision. Without such determination prior to initiating training, supervisors are without guidance on what techniques to teach and may teach a haphazard collection of skills without a unifying theme. A cavalier attitude regarding theory on the part of the instructor/supervisor will likely result in a similar attitude regarding therapy among students/interns. Treatment of clients is likely to suffer as a result.

Beck (1976) offered four standards for evaluating systems of psychotherapy. These may be useful in assessing trainees' understanding and ability to articulate the relationship between the techniques and the theory.

> 1. The system of psychotherapeutic procedures should be well defined and clearly and explicitly described.
> 2. The general principles of treatment should be sufficiently well articulated so that different therapists dealing with the same problem among similar patients can be expected to use similar techniques. Furthermore, the blueprint of therapy should be sufficiently clear and comprehensive so that the neophyte therapist is not forced to proceed like an automaton following the same pat formula for each patient.
> 3. There should be empirical evidence to support the validity of the principles underlying the therapy.
> 4. The efficacy of the treatment should have empirical support, such as: (a) analog studies...; (b) carefully investigated single cases...; (c) well-designed therapeutic trials, (pp. 307-309)

Finally, each intervention will have its own specific techniques which, if described specifically as required to be accepted as a "well-developed system of psychotherapy," will serve as the guideline for assessing a trainee's ability to implement the techniques appropriately.

In summary, at a rudimentary level of assessing competence in interventions (whether psychoanalytic, psychodynamic, behavioral, cognitive, rational-emotive, integrative, transtheoretical, family systems, strategic, whether involving hypnosis or biofeedback, or whether it be brief or long-term) there are six basic questions one should be able to answer.

1. With what modality(ies) has the trainee demonstrated success in implementing the intervention/techniques?

2. With what type of client(s) has the trainee demonstrated success in implementing the intervention/techniques?

3. At what level of complexity is the trainee successfully intervening?

4. Is the trainee able to clearly articulate an understanding of the theory of psychopathology supporting a given intervention?

5. Is the trainee able to clearly articulate an understanding of the relationship between the theory of psychopathology and the system of psychotherapy involved in the intervention?

6. Is the trainee able to demonstrate/implement basic, intermediate, or advanced techniques associated with a given intervention?

Empirically Validated and Supported Treatments

Finally, a task force within Division 12 (Clinical) of APA has promoted the concept of empirically validated and/or supported treatments (see Table 7). Knowledge and skill related to these specific treatments may be considered as elements of the intervention competencies.

Table 7
EXAMPLES OF EMPIRICALLY VALIDATED AND SUPPORTED
TREATMENTS

Beck's cognitive therapy for depression
Behavior modification for developmentally disabled individuals
Interpersonal therapy for bulimia
Klerman and Weissman's interpersonal therapy for depression
Systematic desensitization for simple phobia

From Task Force on Promotion and Dissemination of Psychological Procedures (1993).

Applying Fantuzzo's MASTERY Model

Again, Fantuzzo's (1984) MASTERY model can be used to structure the process of training and evaluating students competency in intervention.

Master Prerequisite Body of Knowledge

As with any area of competence, the scope of knowledge or the ultimate goals of the training need to be clearly specified. Unlike other areas of competence, to have a thorough understanding of all types of interventions, or the available psychotherapies, would generally not be viewed as reasonable or perhaps even beneficial. However, it would be reasonable to expect the student/intern to be able to clearly demonstrate knowledge of at least one psychotherapeutic system and the underlying theory of psychopathology. It is proposed that basic competence in interventions should include, but not necessarily be limited to, the following:

1. Ability to select and articulate understanding of a theory of psychopathology that satisfies the requirements of any good scientific theory. One should be able to explain how the theory addresses basic phenomenon (e.g. developmental process, etc) within its domain with minimal complexity.

2. Ability to clearly define and explicitly articulate the procedures associated with a psychotherapy system so that different therapists dealing with the same problem among similar patients can be expected to use similar techniques.

3. Ability to articulate how the theory of psychopathology is integrally related to its allied psychotherapy system.

4. Ability to articulate knowledge of the effectiveness of the derived psychotherapeutic techniques.

5. Ability to provide verifiable empirical support for the effectiveness of selected interventions to include analogue studies, carefully investigated single case studies, and well-designed therapeutic trials.

6. Ability to provide support of one's effectiveness using the selected intervention.

Assess Skill Competency

Once the scope of competence is defined, the next step is to objectively assess whether or not the trainee can demonstrate the knowledge base as well as application of knowledge and under what circumstances. The following example demonstrates how one might assess intervention competency throughout the internship training year. It is assumed that a level of competency exists on entry into the internship and should increase during the training experience. This format (one and a half to two hours) where the trainee presents a case to a group of psychology supervisors could provide the basic structure. It may be scheduled three to four times throughout the internship training year and could offer ongoing assessment of intervention skills (see Appendix H). A case conference format might include a didactic presentation, audio and/or video tapes and/or other means of demonstrating intervention competency (e.g. live presentation, live observation, etc.). An example of determining intervention competence is provided in Table 8.

Table 8
EXAMPLE – INTERVENTIONS COMPETENCY

1. Discuss understanding of a theory underlying psychopathology associated with intervention to be demonstrated.
2. Define and state the procedures associated with the psychotherapy system.
3. Indicate how the theory of psychopathology is integrally related to its associated psychotherapy system.
4. Review data of the effectiveness of the derived psychotherapeutic techniques.
5. Provide verifiable empirical support for the effectiveness of the therapy selected.
6. Qualify competency by age-limit restrictions.
7. Demonstrate effectiveness using the selected intervention and the following level system:
   A. Individual Therapy
      Level One: The trainee is able to effectively work with a client who presents with a single, focal issue (Axis I only). Effectiveness is demonstrated by positive outcome via patient self-report, rapid assessment instruments, and/or behavioral observations.
      Level Two: The trainee is able to effectively work with a client with cognitive impairment, dual diagnosis, social/familial impairment or complex psychiatric and behavioral deficits. Effectiveness is demonstrated by movement toward or achievement of treatment goals established early in therapy.
      Level Three: The trainee is able to effectively work with a client with a chronic level of psychosis or personality disorders. Effectiveness is demonstrated by evidence of good life adjustment. This level could also be demonstrated by effectively handling an acute suicide intervention or acute psychotic intervention.
   B. Group Therapy
      Level One: The trainee participates as a co-facilitator of a group with a senior staff assuming major responsibility for outcome.

Level Two: The trainee serves as leader of a psychoeducational or highly structured group with high functioning clients/patients. Effectiveness is demonstrated by prepost measures assessing improvement in patient functioning or increase in patient knowledge.

Level Three: The trainee leads a therapy process group with a blend of diverse patients. Effectiveness is demonstrated by positive outcome via patient self-report, rapid assessment instruments, and/or behavioral observations.

Set minimal competency standard: Given the use of a case conference format, and assuming a minimum of three and a maximum of four senior psychology staff reviewing the case, minimum competency would be determined by agreement of two out of three or three out of four staff. For instance, if three out of four staff agree that item #1 of Table 8 had been successfully demonstrated, the competency would be considered met. All seven competencies or limitations would need to be addressed and level documented by the end of the internship year.

Train to Competency

Methods for training to competency would begin with providing the trainee with detailed feedback of strengths as well as deficits from the case conference. Depending on the deficits, the supervisor of record might provide more opportunity to review audio/video tapes with the trainee providing feedback and demonstrating more effective use of said interventions. Self-evaluation with a supervisor present would provide the trainee the opportunity to review their own work against the competencies stated above and compare their review with the supervisor's review. Case conferences would continue until the desired level of competency is achieved.

Chapter 6

TRAINING IN RESEARCH

Research is often both fascinating and anxiety provoking for students. Students are frequently drawn toward the excitement of developing a study, adding to new knowledge in the field, and seeing it presented at either conferences or in a published format. Not all students, though, share that enthusiasm for research which is a central part of basic psychology training (Trierweiler & Stricker, 1991). Those students may be fearful of the process of research and require greater assistance, including increased mentoring, to achieve at the level at which they are capable.

Psychology should develop research training programs which result in learners gaining a basic discernment and respect for the scientific underpinnings of the field as well as an understanding of scientific methodology. Such training will enable them to interpret research findings in addition to designing, carrying out, and reporting on research projects. Training in research is an opportunity for cultivating critical thinking skills in students including observation, logic, and plausible inference (Trierweiler & Stricker, 1991).

The historical importance of research in psychology and how the methods of scientific inquiry have guided research, theory development, and practice are essential components of research training. Basic research curriculum should include statistics, measurement theory, research design, quasiexperimental design, field studies, qualitative methodology, observation, surveys, questionnaires, sociological approaches, and the development of solid writing skills (Trierweiler & Stricker, 1991). In addition to these basic aspects of research, other areas that might be included in the research curriculum are reviewing how confounding events may impact outcome, how selection, such as with volunteers, may restrict generalizability, and how communication of experimenter expectancy can confound results (Cook & Campbell, 1979); developing boundaries for the information to be considered during qualitative studies, understanding of language usage in the local environment, and theories' abilities to be translated at the local level (Miles & Huberman, 1984; Mishler, 1986); the impact of base rates, actuarial versus clinical prediction, and hypothesis testing in clinical cases.

Research Mentoring

The Research Training Environment Scale-Revised (Gelso, Mallinckrodt, & Judge, 1996) was developed to explore the variables which impacted training in research. Kahn and Gelso (1997) found two factors which "accounted for more than half of the variance in the RTES-R" (p. 31). The two factors they found were "interpersonal" and "instructive." The former entails trainees becoming involved with research early in their educational careers as well as faculty modeling appropriate research skills. Early involvement with a faculty member's research appears to be particularly important for women (Krieshok, Somberg, & Cantrell, 1996). Having students involved in research early and continuing on through internship may result in an increased probability of research productivity during the course of their careers, and elevate their understanding and usage of research to guide their clinical treatments.

One particular issue of note regarding Kahn and Gelso's (1997) finding was that early exposure to research should be done in a manner that minimizes the potential for it to be viewed as a threatening experience. Thus, early, gradual teaching/modeling/mentoring of students/trainees is important and may result in elevated research proficiency and output. The other factor found in the research training environment entailed instructional characteristics. This included the obvious such as proper statistics and research design, but also involved realizing that all experiments have some error, how to generate research ideas, developing varied techniques to conduct a study, and the notion that science and direct application can mingle. These instructional goals can be addressed during the doctoral program in addition to the internship and postdoctoral training. To assess a student's sense of self-efficacy regarding research, the Research Attitudes Measure (O'Brien & Lucas, 1993) can be administered. This may be well utilized by internship staff soon after beginning the program to determine which interns may require intense mentoring and at what level they are currently and, therefore, what skills may need to be addressed.

Research During Internship

Depending upon resources and the emphasis of a given internship, training staff may consider either a rotation in research or have it as part of rotations in certain clinical areas. The internship has generally been considered a time to develop clinical skills, however the development of research prowess can be helpful to the future of the trainee. Such skill assists in making decisions about published research and in being a knowledgeable consumer. It also prepares them to play an active role in producing research and evaluating programs, tasks that psychologists may be called upon to perform in greater frequency as the milieu and work arena continue to change. Many interns have had at least rudimentary exposure to research and its related skills. However, they are in need of guidance regarding developing a research strategy for a specific question as well as selecting statistical tests. Also, many students have had little, if any, exposure to qualitative research and internship may provide the opportunity to explore this avenue to conducting inquiries. Furthermore, presenting results in an efficient manner is a skill few interns have mastered. Dissertations are not the norm for the method of dissemination of new information and a different writing style is necessary. Becoming involved with the research that is ongoing in the internship site or developing one's own study are methods of continuing to progress.

Case Approach

Topic areas for interns' seminars regarding research can include experimental design, selecting statistical tests, and exploration of qualitative research. Johnson and Solso (1978) utilized a case approach to the study of research design. They provided examples of studies and then analyzed each in terms of writing style, experimental design, and interpretations. This same technique could be utilized in course work in graduate school and during seminars on internship to increase familiarity with the components of research. Staff could select studies from the current literature and review them with the interns' assistance for possible confounding variables, proper design, clarity of presentation, usefulness to a theory or to the practicing psychologist. Tests could be given to assess understanding of the presented material so it can be applied. These tests can be oral and/or written. It is recommended they be brief and highly practical (e.g., which of the following research designs would be most suitable to explore the following?, etc.).

Skills

Research skills may include designing a study, selecting statistical measures, conducting a qualitative investigation, analyzing the data, and writing the study and submitting for presentation or publication. Competence can be measured in these skill areas by successful performance in each as measured by a committee of staff psychologists. Some of the staff may have expertise in qualitative analysis, others in quantitative, and some may be particularly adept at writing. Each of the aspects of research can be evaluated by the committee prior to going to the next phase. Problem-based learning, the approach to education some medical schools have adopted, may be applicable. Giving a group of interns a research question and having them work together to design, develop, carry out, and write the results of a study may prove to be an effective and efficient means of increasing research skill during internship.

Basic subject areas within research are traditionally taught in psychology graduate programs. Such is not necessarily the case in internships or postdoctoral training programs, however. Many postdoctoral programs in professional psychology do incorporate a research component into their training curriculum. Not all do, though, and it is not clear what degree of actual training in research is offered in those postdocs which require research. Some postdocs may require a specific number of publications, presentations, or completed grant applications to meet the competency requirements for research. This is an objective method of determining outcome and may be appropriate for persons at the postdoctoral level. The perspective among supervisors of postdoctoral trainees may be that these persons have considerable experience and training and what they need now to hone their skills is further opportunity and time. Other possibilities for training at that level, though, may include extensive mentoring by the supervisor. To what journals should this particular manuscript be sent? What journals have a track record of publishing in this area? Is the supervisor aware of a change in philosophy among a given journal regarding suitable topics for publication? Dealing with the frustration of rejections and working with institutional review boards and grant committees are further areas a seasoned researcher can address during postdoctoral training. This type of knowledge base and skills is very beneficial and may assist persons with developing a research career that otherwise would have been less successful. Postdoctoral trainees can be evaluated on some of these issues by having them generate lists of potential journals for a given manuscript, rank the journals for that manuscript and give reasons for the ranking (e.g., suitability of topic, readership works with the specified population, etc.), learning where to search for potential funding sources, learning how to gain information about a particular grant, selecting which grant should be applied for, writing components of a grant application, and if possible, gaining skill in administering a grant (e.g., budgeting, managing records, etc.).

Assessment of skill in each of these areas may be facilitated by objective written tests, essays, group projects, oral reports/discussions, passing an institutional review board with a proposed research project, submission for publication or presentation, and others. As noted previously, each graduate program and internship have the latitude to determine their goals for training. It is then their responsibility to decide how to assess the trainees' knowledge and skills. Research is an area that is more task focused than many within psychology and may be somewhat easier to adapt to a CBET approach.

Example

An example of applying the MASTERY model (Fantuzzo, 1984) to research training on internship demonstrates potential areas for instruction and evaluation. Mastery of the body of knowledge may be determined by brief written objective tests, individual oral examinations, and/or tests based on presented data and how to proceed given that information.

Topics should include determining a sample, differentiating nominal, ordinal, interval, ratio data, developing an experimental design, selecting an appropriate statistical instrument, entering data for analysis, interpreting results, etc.

Assessing skill competency may be accomplished by having a rating scale developed which assesses core skills associated with research. As discussed previously, this may involve having a group of psychologists review research efforts and determine skill level on each area to be measured. The instrument should be a rating scale that allows the rater to document the presence of the key components (e.g., random sampling, appropriate statistical test chosen according to data, data properly entered, etc.).

Setting the minimal competency initially is often unable to be based on empirical evidence as the literature is sparse on CBET and specific psychological competencies or skills such as research. Staff/faculty may need to set an arbitrary threshold and then over time evaluate the necessity of the particular skill to the outcome to determine if raising or lowering the standard is proper. However, giving a standardized instrument and scoring it in a specified manner may require an initial minimal competency rating at 90 percent or higher in order to avoid problems that could be wrought by interpretation of test results based on a lower threshold.

Training to competency can begin by assessing current skill level through live or simulated performance (Fantuzzo, 1984). For research, this may involve having the student evaluate a research report with multiple flaws to determine their ability to note the errors. Following this, feedback is given which is at least partially derived from the rating scale mentioned above. Videotapes of a highly competent model engaging in the processes of developing a research strategy along with stated reasons for choosing a particular experimental methodology are then shown. Videotapes of a less than competent model may be utilized so that students can participate in the critiquing of research skills. This model may make errors in sampling, design, statistical test selection, statistical usage (e.g., not correct for multiple analyses), and interpretation. A lecture should then be provided regarding frequently encountered errors and their correction. At this point, assessment of skill is conducted again.

Legal and ethical principles is a necessary component of research training. A few of the topics to be addressed are research with minors, informed consent, usage of grant funds, and usage of archival data. These, and others, can be assessed through written tests, review of presented scenarios, having students demonstrate how they would handle various proposed dilemmas, and students' actual behavior during the course of the training program while engaging in research.

Reviewing skill level throughout one's professional life can assist in maintaining competence. A wider range of continuing education offerings and assessing knowledge/skill level may play a role in keeping the professional, including faculty/staff, current and performing at a professional level. It is wise to document the competence of faculty/staff to ensure they have demonstrated appropriate skills and can teach those skills to others.

Chapter 7

TRAINING IN CONSULTATION AND EDUCATION

The Vail Conference had a considerable impact on many aspects of training. Some developments which may not be as well known include the focus on evaluation of competencies of students and continued professional development. These may include both consultation and education. Consultation is a collaborative relationship and is an intervention guided by specific procedures and principles in which the psychologist is not directly involved with delivering the services to a given client (Bent, 1991). Psychologists consult with schools, social service agencies, physicians, courts, management in organizations, and many other individuals and groups (Illback, Maher, & Kopplin, 1991). They may be involved with determination of competency to stand trial, to make decisions, or to handle one's own affairs. Psychologists may consult on health issues, stress management, pain, organizational development, classroom placement, or worker satisfaction and productivity.

Consultation and education (teaching, training) can be very similar. Both involve communication of knowledge and/or skill. Education is the guided facilitation by a psychologist for the enhancement of knowledge, skills, and attitudes in a learner (Bent, 1991) whereas consultation may be defined as an interaction between professionals which involves the application of one's expertise to a specific prob-

59

lem (Caplan, 1970). Therefore, skill in providing information to others is an important aspect of training, particularly during internships and postdoctoral residencies.

Greenhalgh and Macfarlane (1997) discussed a competency grid for evidence-based practice. An example of the competencies they included is as follows:

Specific Competence
- achieves "ownership" of proposed changes in practice implements changes
- obtains necessary resources for implementation of change

Potential Competency Training
- communication skills
- motivating others
- teaching others
- presentation skills
- team development
- leadership skills
- financial management and negotiation skills

The above reveals the importance of consultation. The usage of empirically documented treatments is most beneficial in demonstrating one's practice as efficacious and based on the literature. Communicating that information to others is necessary if one is to engage in evidence-based consultation.

Consultation with Mental Health Practitioners

One component of the ability to deliver information of use to consultees can be assessed through the presence and quality of recommendations in reports. All too frequently, reports provide information on the findings and a diagnosis, but do not discuss treatment considerations that would be helpful to the referral source. For instance, if personality testing reveals a likelihood to engage in substance abuse, would the person benefit from substance abuse treatment and should it be inpatient or outpatient? If an individual is found to be exhibiting early signs of a dementia, should a durable power of attorney be considered so that the person's wishes can be fulfilled when the time arises?

The following issues should be considered in the recommendation section of a report (Wolber & Carne, 1993): Are there immediate needs such as suicidal precautions? Is medical intervention necessary? What would be an appropriate type of intervention and what would the goals be? What are the strengths and weaknesses the person would bring to therapy (e.g., good social skills, highly motivated)? What is the most appropriate way for others to interact with the client (e.g., differential reinforcement, supportive, firm)? Are there other services that would be appropriate (e.g., occupational therapy, recreational therapy)? What is the prognosis and anticipated time-line? Is retesting to be done? Competency-based goals can be developed to examine reports for these types of recommendations.

Consulting with Professionals of Other Disciplines

Interaction with other disciplines is an increasingly important part of practice. How does the person-in-training communicate with others? Are they willing to take time to meet, even informally, to discuss treatment? Does their style of communication encourage future interaction? Do they gather adequate information, from staff, the client, records, prior to making recommendations?

Consultation simulations (i.e., role-playing consultations) are useful methods of assessing skill in this area. School psychology has been very active in CBET for behavioral consultation. Pfeiffer (1981) conducted a study evaluating the 'interpersonal effectiveness' and the 'behavioral recommendations' of students who role-played a consultation with research assistants who had memorized a script. Independent judges, doctoral level psychologists, viewed the simulations and rated them on one of the two variables. Interpersonal skill was assessed using a scale of genuineness/self congruence (Truax & Carkhuff, 1967). Recommendations were evaluated using a five-point rating system ranging from "the (consultant) did not offer any specific suggestion(s), plan(s), or recommendation(s)," to "the (consultant) offered one or more specific suggestion(s), plan(s), or recommendation(s)" (Pfeiffer, 1981, p. 63). No difference was found between students who had been recently accepted into graduate school and those in their first year of graduate training on the degree of interpersonal skill in the consultant role. As might be expected, the somewhat more experienced group performed better by prescribing specific recommendations. An interesting finding, though, was that for newly admitted students, a negative correlation was found between interpersonal skill and the generation of behavioral recommendations. Thus, developing rapport appeared to be incompatible with providing useful behavioral recommendations in beginning students. Such might suggest the need to address the relationship competency first in training before attempting to develop other consultation skills.

Pfeiffer's (1981) study demonstrated that consultation can be assessed in a simulation format. It also can be evaluated in terms of actual consultations that were conducted. This may be through direct observation, audio/visual recordings, case presentations, outcomes, and interviews with consultees.

Consultation Stages

Much has been written about consultation from a school psychology perspective. However, the most frequently cited style of CBET school consultation training is behavioral. It consists of four stages: problem identification, problem analysis, intervention, and evaluation (Bergan & Tombari, 1975; Kratochwill, Elliott, & Busse, 1995). Problem identification involves specifying the particular problem to be addressed, negotiating a goal, and defining problems in terms of correcting discrepancies between observed and expected levels of performance (Kaufman, 1971). The competencies required for this stage, as outlined by Kratochwill and Bergan (1978), include being able to directly and accurately record behavior in a naturalistic setting, accurate recording of responses to contrived situations, and analysis of self report.

Problem analysis is the determination that a problem actually exists, selecting variables that may help with changing the behavior, and outlining a plan to change the behavior (Kratochwill & Bergan, 1978). The competencies required for this stage include communicating behavioral goals (e.g., goals must be clear, objective, and complete; frequency, interval, and duration of responses clearly reported).

The third phase of behavioral consultation involves intervention, a plan to directly address the identified behaviors. The competency required at this point is to adequately gauge if the consultee is able to implement the plan. This may involve assessing the consultee's understanding of the procedures, if there is a tendency to short-circuit the plan, and if there are specific legal and/or ethical considerations in the given environment.

The final stage is problem evaluation (Kratochwill & Bergan, 1978). This reviews the plan and its effectiveness. The data collected following implementation of the plan is analyzed. Knowledge of single-subject research design and understanding of the applied behavioral literature are essential elements.

Consultation Training Tools

Sheridan (1992) trained graduate students in behavioral consultation by using written manuals (i.e., Kratochwill & Bergan, 1990), videotaped models, rehearsal, feedback, self-

monitoring, and generalization training. The results suggested successful learning and utilization of consultation skills.
Kratochwill, Elliott, and Busse (1995) reported the use of
assessment tools to evaluate mastery of three stages of behavioral consultation. These include the 47-item Behavioral
Consultation Process Checklist. The Behavioral
Consultation Knowledge Test evaluates knowledge of the
methods of behavioral consultation. It is comprised of 25
short-answer items. The Behavioral Modification Test entails
37 multiple choice and 21 True/False items to evaluate
understanding of behavior modification procedures. The
Knowledge of Behavioral Principles as Applied to Children
is a brief (22-item) version of the original as developed by
O'Dell, Tarler-Benlolo, & Flynn (1979). It has two versions
that allow for pretest and posttest comparisons. The
Behavior Modification Attitude Scale is 20 items in length
and was developed by Musgrove (1974). It evaluates attitudes towards behavior modification using a Likert-type format. The Intervention Rating Profile is a 15-item instrument
to evaluate teachers' willingness to utilize a particular intervention (Martens, Witt, Elliott, & Darveaux, 1985). The
Consultant Evaluation Form (Erchul, 1987; Erchul &
Chewning, 1990) has 12 questions to determine consultee
perceptions of the consultant and the quality of the consultation. The Training Satisfaction Questionnaire (Kratochwill,
VanSomeren, & Sheridan, 1989) consists of nine items to
assess consultants' satisfaction with training in their program
in behavioral consultation. Lastly, the Consultation Training
Scale (Kratochwill, VanSomeren, & Sheridan, 1989) is a tool
similar to the former and is used to gather additional information about satisfaction with training.

Consultation Training Framework

Kratochwill, Elliott, and Busse (1995) developed a CBET
program for teaching behavioral consultation. Prior to train-

ing, the program utilized the Behavioral Consultation Test, Behavior Modification Test, Behavior Modification Attitude Scale, and the Consultation Process Checklist for baseline interviews. Training was then provided and included readings, observations of experienced consultants, seminars (including empathy and listening skills), videotaped sessions, self-evaluation, and supervision sessions. Posttraining assessments included Behavioral Consultation Knowledge Test, Behavior Modification Test, Behavior Modification Attitude Scale, Consultation Process Checklist, Intervention Rating Profile, Consultation Evaluation Form, Training Satisfaction Questionnaire, and Consultant Training Satisfaction Scale. Another instrument that can be utilized is the Problem Identification Checklist developed by Bergan (1977) and modified by Kratochwill and VanSomeren (1984). This tool assesses the presence of specific verbalizations (e.g., to establish antecedents, to review conditions under which behavior occur) during the consultation interview. Further details on the behavioral consultation training and assessment program can be obtained from Kratochwill, Sheridan, Rotto, and Salmon (1991), Sheridan, Salmon, Kratochwill, and Rotto (1992), and Sheridan (1992).

Illback, Maher, and Kopplin (1991) went on to cite skills necessary to this core area. These were to establish a consultation relationship, develop it through relationship skills, gather data through a variety of means (e.g., interviewing, observation, etc.), develop a course of action and gain cooperation from the consultee to proceed, facilitate collaboration with various stakeholders, assess intervention, and use various techniques including didactic and process groups to communicate information. Attitudes toward consultation are important variables and developing tolerance of ambiguity when making intervention decisions is necessary (Illback, Maher, & Kopplin, 1991). One must also address believing in the ability of the organization to change, and maintaining professionalism during stressful situations. Course work in this area is recommended to include both lecture and field-work-type experiences (Illback, Maher, & Kopplin, 1991). This would allow for the dissemination of the knowledge base as well as an opportunity to develop skills. Facilitators would also be able to measure attitudes during field experiences and address them as necessary. Fieldwork should address the analysis of systems, consultation procedures, and a small group project in consultation in the community or university.

MASTERY: An Approach to Consultation Training

Mastery of a body of knowledge of consultation will depend upon the consultation style that is chosen. If one selected the behavioral method, the Behavior Modification Test would be appropriate to administer as would the Behavioral Consultation Knowledge Test.

Assessing skill competency may involve the utilization of some of the instruments previously mentioned. These include Truax and Carkhuff's (1967) scale of genuineness/self-congruence to assess interpersonal effectiveness, a checklist of behavioral recommendations, Behavioral Consultation Process Checklist, and the Consultant Evaluation Form.

Setting minimal competency must be done by the staff at the training site and obviously will differ depending upon the techniques for evaluation chosen, degree of emphasis placed on various skills, etc.

Training to competency can occur with initial evaluation of skill level possibly using simulated consultations. Feedback is then provided followed by live and videotaped modeling of appropriate consultation behavior. A lecture may then follow on common pitfalls of consultation. Finally, reassessment occurs.

Evaluating the legal and ethical principles involved in consultation may address who the client is, confidentiality, staying within boundaries of competence, and legal/ethical responsibility given specific situations that may arise when providing services as a consultant but not providing direct client services.

Reviewing skill level can entail periodic reassessment of consultation skill level. This may take the form of assessing client perception and satisfaction with the consultation process and outcome.

Education

As noted previously, education is guided assistance to strengthen another's knowledge, skills, and attitudes (Bent, 1991). CBET is a unique method of education and, thus, places a novel set of demands upon the instructor. This section will review the process others have utilized to begin using CBET in their institutions. By doing so, the educator and future-educator may have a foundation upon which to begin the process of utilizing CBET in their educational activities.

Smith and Fuller (1996) detailed the foundational competencies for the Brown University School of Medicine. They identified nine areas of competence they wished their students to meet that were basic to successful lifelong competence as a physician. These can be adjusted to be pertinent to psychology.

- Effective communication
- Basic relationship skills
- Using basic psychological science in practice
- Diagnosis, intervention, consultation
- Lifelong learning
- Self-awareness, self-care, and personal growth
- The community context of psychological intervention
- Ethical judgment
- Problem solving

There are various methods of conducting a review of one's current educational curriculum (Greenwood, Lewis, & Burgess, 1998). Such a review can be done by having faculty and students evaluate the current curriculum and determining how well it prepares one for routine practice. Another method is to use external methods such as performance on licensing examinations. A third method is to examine what professionals do in actual practice and determine if and how the curriculum prepares students for those tasks. An additional method is to project what professionals will be doing in the field mid-way through the student's career and attempt to prepare for such an eventuality. This might be done by examining trends and adjusting the curriculum to include courses and experience in areas likely to be impacted. For example, in the late 1970s to early 1980s one may have been able to anticipate an increased involvement with corporate mental health and multidisciplinary teams and assisted students with consultation skills, treatment plan writing, and organizational expertise. At present, some may project a greater need for understanding of biochemical substrates of behavior. Such may be assisted through coursework in neuroanatomy, biochemistry of behavior, and psychopharmacology.

However, predicting what may be an important new development in professional psychology in 20 years is difficult. The field may go in new and unanticipated directions and students are best served by preparing them to be lifelong learners. Assisting them with developing an interest in teaching themselves through less emphasis on lectures and more on problem-focused learning, projects, autotutorials, conducting research, attendance at conferences, and teaching others may result in psychologists who are able to adapt and change throughout the course of their careers.

Fields that have specific core skills (e.g., dentistry), lend themselves well to a competency approach to education. Fields with less easily observable and measurable skills may necessitate a greater time commitment to the process of converting to a CBET program. The development of a competency-based curriculum is not something achieved in a short period of time. Many months to years may be required to reach an understanding and agreement on the competencies to be demonstrated by the students of a particular institution as well as the methods of evaluation.

The Baylor Experience

McCann, Babler, and Cohen (1998) detailed the milestones in developing a competency-based curriculum at Baylor College of Dentistry. The college committed themselves to a competency-based educational program in January of 1993. This was due to trends in dental education and the movement of the American Association of Dental Schools from a discipline-based curriculum to one that was competency-based. The college had as its goal a "competency-based curriculum (which) provides an education for students that develop skills they need to successfully enter into their profession and instill within them an understanding of their role and responsibility in the health delivery team....There will be a decrease in didactic instruction and an increase in small group and active experiences that will promote lifelong learning....It should place more emphasis on the mentoring/modeling role of the faculty and the clinical learning environment should closely match the practice of dentistry" (McCann, Babler, & Cohen, 1998, p. 201).

Initially, the college reviewed CBET programs at other dental institutions. A draft was then developed to gain initial input from faculty. Eight interdisciplinary faculty teams were then developed and charged with creating competencies thought to be appropriate for their graduates (McCann, Babler, & Cohen, 1998). These teams completed a new draft and sent it to faculty for review. Input was gained and the document was revised. The final document was divided into six domains, 20 major competencies, and 136 supporting competencies.

Following the completion of this document, a new team was established to develop what were known as foundation statements. These would delineate the biomedical, behavioral, and preclinical science content of the curriculum which provided the basis for the eventual completion of each competency. A Director of Assessment was named. This individual organized a team of persons to develop and maintain the assessments required to evaluate competency. The Director of Assessment also asked faculty to complete a survey of importance of course content in developing each supporting competency in order to determine where the competencies were being gained in the curriculum.

A revision occurred based on the curriculum review and this resulted in 120 supporting competencies as opposed to the earlier 136. Various tools were used to determine the effectiveness of the curriculum. These included: grades and performance assessments, Western Regional Board Examination, National Board Examination, patient satisfaction surveys, survey of seniors in the program, graduation survey (self-assessment), faculty and group leader surveys, survey of alumni, student course evaluations, focus groups with students and/or faculty, review by curriculum committee, and monitoring by strategic planning committee.

Ethics was an important component of the Baylor program. The college assessed it through written examinations in various courses. Written case analyses were also methods of ethics evaluation as were auditing of records, infection control evaluation, group leader evaluation of professionalism, and self-evaluation of professionalism. Such a framework could easily be adopted for use by psychology. Ethics could be assessed during coursework, review of case records, oral response to presented scenarios, and practicum supervisor reviews. The initial decision to adopt a CBET model at Baylor's dental program was in January of 1993. The competency document was revised and completed in 1997. The college began a self-study in 1997 and anticipated being reviewed by the Southern Association of Colleges and Schools in 1999.

LESSONS LEARNED. The Baylor College of Dentistry, during their efforts to adopt a CBET model, learned the importance of involving faculty. They were involved in competency course surveys, self-studies, and using evaluation data to improve education.

It was imperative that faculty understood the difference between discipline-based and competency-based training. In addition, the groups responsible for planning the curriculum and outlining the competencies must have regular communication with those responsible for assessment. Without such linkage, planning is without a direction and assessment may test skills not related to the end goal. McCann, Babler, and Cohen (1998) stated that multiple assessment strategies must be used. Competency should not be signified by passing one test on one occasion using one technique or modality. The "performance selected for evaluation should closely resemble the skill or competency as it is performed" (p. 204) in clinical practice. Faculty determine if a student may graduate based on the student's readiness for independent practice, not on the student's having completed a sequence of courses.

Faculty were concerned about issues pertaining to their own competence (e.g., responsibility for "problems" noted, potential changes in teaching methods and courses taught). While it is likely that faculty will initially feel uncomfortable with changes in the educational model, the Baylor staff found that as the alteration developed, faculty members began to own the process and ask for more data on which to make decisions about the curriculum.

McCann, Babler, and Cohen (1998) described the optimal order of changing to a CBET model. The first is to define the competencies. What is it the institution wishes students to be able to do when they leave? The second is measure the competencies. Develop techniques to assess those competencies. Finally, alter the curriculum to teach the competencies you wish to measure. Any other order would likely prevent or at least inhibit the successful implementation of a CBET model.

Assessment Center

Continuing education has tended to use only didactic workshops and conferences. Fordyce & Meier (1987) discussed a competency-based approach for persons already in the field and desiring new training. They advocated the usage of the Assessment Center, a methodology of evaluation having different modules for assessment in a central location. It has been used in management selection and placement programs in corporations and in some of the divisions of the American Board of Professional Psychology. Hill, Stalley, Pennington, Besser, and McCarthy (1997) used a similar approach with medical students to teach and assess skill in managing trauma cases. Fordyce and Meier (1987) suggested this could be used with a variety of topics in psychology (e.g., systematic desensitization). Once completely developed, such a center could serve as an "open-ended postdoctoral program without extended absence from professional practice," (p. 409). Such a model could be an excellent addition to the traditional didactic means of providing information for continuing education. As Fordyce and Meier stated, the components of a particular task are broken down into question banks and work sample simulations. Autotutorial and small group educational exercises are provided to guide the learner toward obtaining the knowledge, attitudes, and skills required for a given task.

Consultation and Education: Some Final Thoughts

Psychologists often provide in-service training to various disciplines and colleagues. Teaching can go beyond the classroom and include interdisciplinary team meetings and patient education. Educational facilitation opportunities will

continue to increase as psychology grows and reaches a larg-
er arena and continues to become more specialized (Illback,
Maher, & Kopplin, 1991). These authors cite the core competencies in psychology as related to consultation and education. These involve an understanding of the historical
developments of the community mental health movement
and community psychology to include primary, secondary,
and tertiary intervention; characteristics of populations for
whom non-traditional services may be appropriate; group,
social, and organizational psychology concepts; an appreciation for the mechanisms of service delivery and the environment in which they operate (e.g., regulatory agencies, social
services, corrections, managed care, etc.); human-environ-
ment interaction, and understanding of consultation principles.

Many institutions offer the opportunity for students to
develop teaching skills through serving as a teaching assis-
tant. Also, students typically give many presentations in
class during the course of their graduate program, thus gaining some experience in presentation of knowledge in a
didactic setting. A course in consultation and education
would be able to emphasize teaching skills and methodology. This may include lesson planning, usage of audio/visual
aids, facilitating class discussion, distance-learning, tele-
health, and gathering feedback. These skills will be useful
regardless of the primary service area of the psychologist.

Chapter 8

TRAINING IN SUPERVISION

Supervision is a necessary component of a psychologist's skill repertoire. Though viewed as a basic clinical competency by the NCSPP in 1989 and as an aspect of practice that may become more prominent (Spruill, Kohout, & Gehlmann, 1997) in the evolving healthcare marketplace, the amount of literature addressing the means of training doctoral students, interns, and postdoctoral students in the provision of supervision is quite limited. Research examining training practices (e.g., Scott, Ingram, Vitanza, & Smith, 1998) reveals the lack of a prescribed program for training supervisors, and offers little guidance for developing competency-based supervision training programs.

TRAINING IN SUPERVISION: AN ISSUE OF INCREASED IMPORTANCE

The practice of supervision in the twenty-first century will be influenced by research trends and external influences (see Watkins, 1998). An American Psychological Association (APA) working group (Spruill, Kohout, & Gehlmann, 1997) highlighted the changes that may occur in the practice area of psychology, and suggested that changes in service delivery systems would translate into psychologists spending more time engaged in the provision of supervision.

Members of the training community obviously consider the preparation of their students as supervisors as an important element of the graduate education in professional psychology. Scott, Ingram, Vitanza, and Smith (1998), in a survey of APA-Accredited doctoral and internship programs, found that trainees viewed training in supervision as an aspect of training that is of increasing importance due to the recent changes in the healthcare system.

Supervision Training Practices

Though trainers view proficiency in supervision as a fundamental clinical skill, the pathway to achieving competency in this area of practice is unclear. Scott et al. (1998) surveyed 123 doctoral programs and 209 internship sites to learn of their supervision practices. In doctoral programs, didactic instruction, tape review, group discussions of supervision practices, individual supervision of supervision, and assigned readings were utilized at similar rates. Didactic instruction was the most common training practice used to train interns. Audio/videotape review of supervision sessions was a component of only 24 percent of the internship programs.

Means of assessing training outcome and students' supervision skills are varied, but verbal feedback appears to be the most commonly-used evaluation tool (Scott et al., 1998). Approximately 14 percent of programs, doctoral and internship combined, that provided training did not conduct evaluations of their students' performance.

Supervision is an intervention that enhances the professional functioning of students/junior professionals, monitors the quality of professionals services provided, and functions as a gatekeeping mechanism for the profession (Bernard & Goodyear, 1992). As with counseling and psychotherapy, the complexity of this clinical skill presents trainers who are striving towards competency-based training with numerous questions. What are the basic components of competent supervision practice? What training methods promote these basic competencies? How are these competencies evaluated?

The answers to those questions are not readily available. The professional literature addressing the basic elements of quality supervision is limited. Stoltenberg (1981), in his application of a cognitive development theory (Hunt, 1971), posited that there were two specific skill areas important for effective supervision: discrimination and creating environments. The effective supervisor should be able to discriminate between interventions that give the supervisee varying degrees of support and guidance, and should be able to identify the supervisee's strengths and weaknesses and tailor interventions to the supervisee. Creating environments allows the supervisee to receive the appropriate amount of structure and guidance dependent upon their skill level. Wampold and Holloway (1997) described key supervision elements within their causal model of research. Supervisor and supervisee characteristics, as they relate to each other and the supervision process, are the components of the model. Review of these descriptions of supervision and others lead to the conclusion that the key components of supervision have not yet been defined with specificity. Thus, the basic components of competent supervision are not defined.

The training methods for evaluating supervision competency are quite diverse, as indicated by the results of Scott et al. (1998). Formalized or routinized methods for evaluating supervision competency are not commonly used in training settings. Are they available? Beyond the performance questionnaires commonly used by training programs, few competency checklists or evaluation tools are available. Given the complexity of the clinical skill area and the limitations in currently used training methods and evaluation tools, is competency-based training in supervision a realistic ideal? Though it may be difficult to actualize, it is important that the training community strives for this ideal. The MASTERY model (see Table 9) may provide a framework for developing a competency-based training system focused on enhancing and assessing supervision skills.

A NOTE ABOUT MANAGEMENT. Management, a competency area suggested by NCSPP (1989), is comprised of activities that direct, organize, and control the services that psychologists and other professionals provide. Considering the developmental process that a psychologist must go through to establish competency in management, supervision competency seems to be a prerequisite for the development of case management and administrative proficiency. Thus, competency-based training in the broader area of management becomes the responsibility of the internships and postdoctoral trainers. More focus on management in the training literature is needed as training practices in this area are not well defined.

Table 10
COMPONENTS OF THE MASTERY MODEL FOR TRAINING
SUPERVISORS

Master Prerequisite Body of Knowledge

Student completes coursework and/or assigned reading in supervision models, techniques, and processes.
Student passes tests or qualifying examinations over the material.
Student views videotapes that portray expert supervisors demonstrating basic skills.
Student completes lab sessions that focus on the development of basic supervision skills.

Assess Skill Competency

Student conducts 3-5 supervision sessions with confederate supervisees (other students) presenting different supervision scenarios.
Trainer reviews videotape of supervision sessions and provides immediate verbal and written feedback to the student.
Trainer evaluates student skills with a questionnaire or checklist.

Set Minimal Competency Standard

Trainer sets a clear competency standard as determined by tape review/performance measure.

Train to Competency

Trainer presents a lecture on the specific application of supervision skills.
Student views videotape of an expert supervising confederates presenting the supervision scenarios originally presented to the students.

Student completes supervision session with supervisees that are reviewed in group supervision of supervision.

Evaluate Understanding of Relevant Ethical and Legal Principles

Trainer presents a lecture on ethical and legal issues related to supervision.
Student obtains a passing grade on a quiz over ethical and legal principles.

Review Skill Level

Student supervision skills are reevaluated periodically.

Yield to Continuing Education

Trainers provide students with continuing education information and opportunities.

Chapter 9

TRAINING IN ADVANCED
SPECIALTY AREAS

The graduate curriculum should ideally be 60 percent foundational with the remainder addressing specialties or special emphasis areas (Bent, 1991). The first year of the doctoral program is to be foundational in nature with the second year involving a mix of foundational material and specialty area interests. Year three can emphasize specialties. Internship may allow for some pursuit of specialties, but specialization should take place at the postdoctoral level (Bent, 1991).

Psychology appears to be developing an increased number of specialties. The American Board of Professional Psychology in recent years has gone from offering diplomas in clinical, counseling, and school, to many others including rehabilitation, family, and behavioral psychology. CBET can be developed by experts in these areas and utilized predoctorally and during postdoctoral training.

Specialty Training Models

Disciplines other than psychology have been using CBET for some time. Their experience may offer guidance on how psychology can begin to advance this philosophy of education within its own training settings. Hill, Stalley, Pennington,

Besser, and McCarthy (1997) addressed CBET for medical students by developing a system of teaching and assessing one's understanding of treating medical emergencies. Their program involved a study guide which detailed the competencies to be mastered and how that was best done. Teaching modules were developed to provide knowledge basic to carrying out the necessary duties of dealing with trauma patients. After each teaching session, an evaluation occurred in the form of multiple choice, group clinical examination, or short answer questions. Their program was based on the acronym of SCORPIO which stood for structured, clinical, objective-referenced, problem-based, integrated, and organized. Students were divided into small groups and each group rotated through six teaching stations lasting 25 minutes each. A teacher at each station conducted an interactive lecture addressing a specific competency. One of the series addressed a multidisciplinary approach to neurotrauma. Neurosurgeons conducted the stations on care of hematoma and spinal injury, another physician conducted the station on cerebral edema, a neuropsychologist presented an actual patient with cognitive impairment for discussion on head injury rehabilitation, while a physiatrist demonstrated the various aspects of function in persons with spinal injury at the final station. Students later were assessed using a 30-station Objective Structured Clinical Examination (OSCE). The standard assessment station involved a written vignette or a manikin or other visual source. Students were expected to perform a clinical skill or respond to a series of open-ended, short-answer questions, typically related to some feature of patient management. Scores may be assigned to responses to questions pertaining to tests ordered, diagnosis, dealing with complications, treatment options, and relapse prevention. Hill et al. found that persons trained in this manner performed better during OSCE examinations than persons trained in a more traditional manner.

Training Models in Specialty Areas of Psychology

Smith and Fuller (1996) described the CBET program at Brown University School of Medicine. They presented a matrix which addressed certain competency domains (e.g., maintenance and homeostasis) and application areas (e.g., single organ, whole person). Table 10 is presented as a demonstration for its applicability to specialty areas in psychology, in this case, neuropsychology.

Table 10
COMPETENCY MATRIX FOR NEUROPSYCHOLOGY

Neuroanatomy
Clinical Neurology
Neuropathology

Instruments_____

	Diagnosis	Acute	Chronic	Children	Adolescents	Geriatric
Testing						
Scoring						
Interpretation						
Diagnosis (skill)						
Patient Care						
Treatment						
Research						
Writing						
Consulting						

This type of competency grid can be used to see that an individual has attained the necessary experiences and has had a broad array of diagnoses (e.g., traumatic brain injury, Alzheimer's Disease) and variation of recency of onset and age. Such a grid could be developed for a variety of specialty areas. One for biofeedback might include the information contained in Table 11.

It is obvious that individual competencies would need to be developed, taught, and evaluated for each area within the total grid. However, the above may provide basic direction when considering overall goals for a biofeedback training experience.

Table 11
COMPETENCY GRID FOR BIOFEEDBACK

	Anxiety	Headache	TMJ	CLB	PTSD	Substance abuse	ADD
Clinical interview							
Diagnosis							
Psychotherapy							
Physiology							
Pain management							
Health psychology							
Psychophysiology							
Instrumentation							
Application of	EMG						
	Temp						
	EDG						
	EEG						
Treatment planning							
Relapse Prevention							

For example, one area that is becoming an increasingly stronger facet of applied psychology is geropsychology. Education and training of psychologists to work with the elderly may involve an understanding of the complexity of the related interpersonal, social, and health problems. Students should be exposed to the healthy as well as the frail older adults and to recognize normal and pathological aging (Knight, Santos, Teri, & Lawton, 1995). Students should be given exposure to working with the elderly in their homes, senior centers, nursing homes, and hospitals. Role changes, loss, developmental crises, suicide, ageism, retirement, memory alterations, and social skills difficulties should all be addressed in a training program (Knight, Santos, Teri, & Lawton, 1995; Logsdon, 1995). Neuropsychology with the usage of proper norms, family systems, health psychology, reminiscence therapy, and psychopharmacology are further areas of required competence for a geropsychologist. Case studies (e.g., Knight, 1992) can be used to explore many of these issues within the older adult. Psychopharmacology and the elderly should address drug absorption, distribution, metabolism, elimination, interactions with other medications, common side effects, prevalence of drug usage, heightened susceptibility to adverse effects, and the omission from many drug development studies (Smyer & Downs, 1995). In addition, issues of medication compliance and the difficulty of managing a complex regimen should be reviewed.

Specialty areas of psychology have their own instruments and/or procedures to utilize which require competence to utilize. Neuropsychologists may use various instruments to assess visuospatial functioning, abstraction, and language skills. Health psychologists may use instruments to evaluate pain or the impact of psychological variables on health status. Competency standards could be developed for each area to be assessed within a specialty. Blakey, Fantuzzo, and Moon (1985) used a training program to teach doctoral students to competently administer the Wechsler Adult Intelligence Scale-Revised (WAIS R). Evaluation of competence was made by using the Criteria for Competent WAIS-R Administration (CCWA) (Fantuzzo & Moon, 1984), which was a checklist of 177 items in 14 sections. Examples include beginning with item 5 on the Information subtest if appropriate, reading questions verbatim, and avoiding evaluative comments.

Specific characteristics of CBET include a curriculum that is based on actual tasks the student will encounter as a professional, is directed at a specific role and setting, addresses performance outcomes, and is based on clear competency statements (Alspach, 1984). In addition, Alspach required publication of the expectations of students, flexibility in how teaching is conducted, evaluation methods being criterion-referenced, assisting student remediation as necessary, and being learner centered. This demonstrates why each individual site will find it necessary to examine their philosophy of education and what they are attempting to teach and why a universal CBET plan cannot be used across programs. Medical centers in Boston and New York may both have postdoctoral training programs in neuropsychology. However, philosophy of assessment may be the process approach, hypothesis testing, or fixed battery. Also, one site may greatly emphasize research while another may emphasize clinical duties. Sites that encourage research may have variations on where research should be published or presented or the focus of research (e.g., specific diseases, tests, or age groups, be clinically focused or address general experimental neuropsychological issues, use case studies or large samples, etc.). CBET can help ensure that students learn what the sites have determined is important.

It is obvious why degree-granting institutions or training sites must explore their goals for education and develop competencies for each. It is this variation that will keep psychology from producing a series of clones, graduates with the exact same skills taught in the same manner. This variation will also assist in keeping psychology from becoming a field of technicians. CBET is a tool that has the potential to result in better skilled graduates. Establishing competencies and assessment procedures must not be the end of our efforts, though. To meet the spirit of CBET, regular reassessment of what needs to be learned as well as the reevaluation of programs needs to occur. The competency areas must serve as a "flexible guide" (Bent, 1991, p. 77) for curriculum development. It is up to each institution which provides education and training to be vigilant to changes in the field and in educational practices so as to provide relevant and meaningful instruction to the learners who are investing themselves in this field.

Chapter 10

TRAINING IN ETHICS

ETHICS AND ATTITUDES

Before one can begin to assess competency in ethics, "ethics" must first be defined. Many professional psychologists when confronted with the question of defining "ethical behavior" are likely to espouse the profession's code of conduct (Ethical Principles for Psychologists and Code of Conduct, APA, 1992). Why not, since each year, incoming graduate students are likely to be handed a copy (or directed to *www.apa.org* where a copy can now be downloaded) to read, study, and maybe even memorize? However, do the Ethical Principles "define" ethics?

Diener and Crandell (1978) define ethics as the "expressions of our values and guide for achieving them." Values, then, are viewed as the underpinnings of ethical principles (Eberliein, 1996) and are defined as principles or qualities that are intrinsically desirable (Mish, 1985). Ethics, then, cannot be understood separate from an understanding of the value system on which they are based. What behaviors do we value? What ideals do we value?

Recent literature has debated the value of two seemingly disparate approaches to ethics. On the one hand, *principle ethics* have been defined as a "set of prima facie obligations one considers when confronted with an ethical dilemma," (Meara, Schmidt, & Day, 1996, p. 4) or "approaches that emphasize the use of rational, objective, universal, and

85

impartial principles in the ethical analysis of dilemmas" (Jordan & Meara, 1996). Principle ethics address the question of "What shall I do?" or how should I act when confronted with a given situation. Principle ethics reveal the behaviors we value as a profession.

Conversely, *virtue ethics* focus on "character traits and non-obligatory ideals that facilitate the development of ethical individuals" (Meara, Schmidt, & Day, 1996, p. 4) and are "characterized by an emphasis on historical virtues" (Jordan & Meara, 1996). In other words, ethics that dictate "Who shall I be?" as opposed to "What shall I do?." Virtue ethics place the emphasis on educating professionals toward being a certain type of person (e.g., competent, honest, etc.) as opposed to training them how to perform under given situations. Virtue ethics define the ideal "character" we value as individuals.

Meara and her colleagues (Meara, Schmidt, & Day, 1996, p. 4) call for an integration of these two types of ethics, stating that a "focus on human character, or the questions of who or what we and our ideals are, becomes inextricably linked to our actions" (p. 49). This would suggest that one's ethics are not merely how one responds (i.e., proscribed behavior) to an ethical dilemma but rather how one enacts (i.e., attitude) their view of themselves and their ideals (Oehlert, Sumerall, & Lopez, 1998). In fact, the Ethical Principles contain both virtue ethics (General Principles) and principle ethics (Ethical Standards).

Bernard and Jara (1995) note two elements crucial to graduate students failing to apply ethical guidelines: (1) lack of knowledge or understanding of the principle, and (2) degree of unwillingness to conform to the principle. This suggests that in order to produce competent ethical professionals, we cannot rely entirely on just teaching the principles, but must also fully assess the likelihood that trainees are willing to conform to the principle. Thus, it is not enough to know the principles, they must be willing to implement them.

Finally, what is one to do when confronted with a situation where the application of one principle conflicts with the application of another principle. Even APA recognizes that the ethical standards and principles are not sufficiently detailed to alleviate ethical dilemmas. Dilemmas occur when a situation presents one with more than one good reason to take different courses. For instance, what should one do when the law suggests one response and ethical guidelines propose a conflicting response? (Pope & Bajt, 1988; Ansell & Ross, 1988; Eenwyk, 1988; Kalichman, 1990; & Bersoff, 1975). Or perhaps more basic, what does one do when to endorse one ethical principle violates a subsequent principle? How does one determine the most appropriate "decision making " process for resolving ethical dilemmas? (Kitchener, 1986; & Pelsma & Borgers, 1986; Eberlein, 1986). Competence in ethical decision making requires that one have a reasonable decision-making process to anchor decisions when confronted with a dilemma.

In summary, then, it is recommended that any measure of ethical competence should include three major components. First, trainees should have knowledge of both *principle ethics* and *virtue ethics*. Secondly, there should be a means of assessing willingness or openness to applying the ethical guidelines. Finally, competence is not complete without a reasonable plan for resolving ethical dilemmas.

Application of MASTERY Model

Master Prerequisite Body of Knowledge

It is proposed that basic ethical competence should include, but not necessarily be limited, to the following:

1. Understand and apply the *Ethical Principles of Psychologists and Code of Conduct* (APA, 1992; see Appendix I).

2. Understand and apply knowledge of ethical decision-making processes (see Appendices J & K).
3. Articulate one's own values and virtues in terms of one's personal ethics.

Assess Knowledge and Skill Competency

Once the scope of competence is defined, the next step is to objectively assess whether or not competence has been achieved. There are a variety of ways to assess competency in any area. While "examinations" may be the best way to assess knowledge base, it is not necessarily the most appropriate means of assessing the application of knowledge. The following example (Table 12) utilizes both assessment of knowledge and assessment of application of basic competency in ethics. Using the internship year as the training period, it is assumed that mastery of basic knowledge should be present on entry into the internship.

Table 12
EXAMPLE – ASSESSMENT OF ETHICAL KNOWLEDGE

Part I. Internship - Entry level Assessment:
  1. Demonstrate knowledge of the *Ethical Principles of Psychologists and Code of Conduct* (APA, 1992), (see Appendix I for Sample Test).
    A. Identify six general principles.
    B. Identify eight categories of ethical standards.
    C. Identify statements as included (or not) in the code of ethics.
  2. Demonstrate knowledge of ethical decision-making processes. (See Appendix J)
    A. Kitchener (1984) five fundamental ethical principles.
    B. Redlich and Pope (1985) seven principles for confronting dilemmas.
    C. Keith-Spiegel and Kooch (1987) Problem-Solving approach.
    D. Rest (1983) four components of moral behavior.
  3. Minimal Competency Standard on Knowledge is 95-100%. It is assumed that to not know some part of the Ethical Principles or to be unaware of basic ethical decision-making processes will make it difficult, if not impossible, to fully demonstrate ethical behavior.
  4. Methods for training to competency at the knowledge level would include providing literature, training seminar as needed, and test/retest opportunities.

Assessment of Ethical Skill
  1. Define personal "virtue" ethics and how they are integrated in one's ethical decision-making process. This exericse could be one either dependently or independently of a specific case presentation. Independently, in a seminar presentation, members of a training class might each present in written and/or oral format their "virtue" ethics and the decision-making process they will utilize in making ethical choices.
  2. Demonstrate ability to apply ethical principles to a variety of dilemmas.
      Pope and Vetter (1992) describe 703 ethically troubling incidents reported by members of APA. Most troubling were those involving confidentiality (18%); blurred, dual, or conflictual relationships (17%); payment sources, plans, settings, and methods (14%); academic settings, teaching dilemmas and concerns about training (8%); and forensic psychology (5%). Vignettes describing these dilemmas could be presented to trainees. Ideas for vignettes can be gleaned from resources such as Bersoff (1995) and Kitchener (1984). Using the checklist based on Rest's model of moral behavior (see Appendix C), trainees should attain 90-100% as a minimal standard of competency.
  3. Demonstrate ethical behavior in ongoing therapy/assessment/supervision cases.
      Monthly, a random case could be selected by the supervisor and presented by the trainee. Using the Checklist (Appendix K) trainees should attain 90-100% of the items as fours or fives as a minimum standard of competency.
  4. Minimum Standard for Competency—Using the ethics checklist (see Appendix K) minimum competency standard is 90-100%.
  5. Training for Competency—It is generally agreed that ethical training does not happen merely by osmosis (Handlesman, 1986), rather it requires a deliberate training effort. Rest's model which is used in the checklist can also be used to identify areas of deficiency. Training can then be focused on those specific areas and may include literature, role-playing, vignettes, etc. Vasquez (1992) offers specific tips to supervisors on how to promote ethical practice including the use of guided imagery.

EPILOGUE

This book has attempted to provide an introduction to competency-based training for those who are involved with the education of psychology students. CBET has been utilized in various disciplines including subfields of psychology. However, its widespread use in psychology has only recently been mandated. We have introduced the concept to major areas of training and its usage is likely to expand.

As the field progresses with CBET, there will be increased information on how to define, teach, and assess competency. It is our hope that the field and those whom are served are benefitted by this change. However, we believe it is imperative that flexibility in what is taught and how training occurs within a given program remain an integral component of CBET.

APPENDIX A

CULTURAL SENSITIVITY SELF REPORT

(Lopez, 1996)

Please reflect upon your work with clients when responding to the following statement. Circle the appropriate rating for each item.

1. Stereotyping is done by counselors, even well-intentioned ones.

Strongly Agree   Moderately Agree   Neutral   Moderately Disagree   Strongly Disagree

2. Ethnicity, marital status, parental status, socioeconomic status, religious affiliation, gender, sexual orientation, and geographic affiliation should be considered when forming a conceptualization of a client.

Strongly Agree   Moderately Agree   Neutral   Moderately Disagree   Strongly Disagree

3. I am willing to refine my clinical hypotheses as pertinent cultural information is presented.

Strongly Agree   Moderately Agree   Neutral   Moderately Disagree   Strongly Disagree

4. An accurate clinical picture of the client can be developed without purposely applying culturally relevant information to the conceptualization.

Strongly Agree   Moderately Agree   Neutral   Moderately Disagree   Strongly Disagree

5. I am willing to acquire knowledge of cultural variables to create an accurate view of a client in an ideographic perspective.

Strongly Agree   Moderately Agree   Neutral   Moderately Disagree   Strongly Disagree

6. I am motivated to engage in self-exploration in order to identify biases and prejudices.

Strongly Agree   Moderately Agree   Neutral   Moderately Disagree   Strongly Disagree

7. One's culture influences the counseling.

   Strongly Agree   Moderately Agree   Neutral   Moderately Disagree   Strongly Disagree

8. The conceptualization of a case should remain flexible, so incoming cultural data can be incorporated.

   Strongly Agree   Moderately Agree   Neutral   Moderately Disagree   Strongly Disagree

9. Intentional use of cultural data is one aspect of effective treatment.

   Strongly Agree   Moderately Agree   Neutral   Moderately Disagree   Strongly Disagree

10. Cultural information gathered about the client needs to be considered as a factor when planning interventions and treatment.

    Strongly Agree   Moderately Agree   Neutral   Moderately Disagree   Strongly Disagree

11. The cross-cultural client will unknowingly present all culturally relevant information needed for facilitating effective cross-cultural counseling.

    Strongly Agree   Moderately Agree   Neutral   Moderately Disagree   Strongly Disagree

12. I consider myself value-free when I am engaged in the counseling process.

    Strongly Agree   Moderately Agree   Neutral   Moderately Disagree   Strongly Disagree

13. A power differential exists in the counseling relationship and impacts perceptions of culture.

    Strongly Agree   Moderately Agree   Neutral   Moderately Disagree   Strongly Disagree

14. Ethnicity is the only characteristic that should be considered when conceptualizing cross-cultural clients.

    Strongly Agree   Moderately Agree   Neutral   Moderately Disagree   Strongly Disagree

15. My personal biases and prejudices will not influence my relationship with cross-cultural clients.

    Strongly Agree   Moderately Agree   Neutral   Moderately Disagree   Strongly Disagree

16. A counselor and a cross-cultural client are on equal footing, and collaboration is easily facilitated.

    Strongly Agree   Moderately Agree   Neutral   Moderately Disagree   Strongly Disagree

APPENDIX B

EMPATHIC UNDERSTANDING IN
INTERPERSONAL PROCESSES

[Carkuff as presented by C. H. Patterson (1974), pp. 54-55]

Level One–The verbal and behavior expressions of the first person either do not attend to or detract significantly from the verbal and behavioral expressions of the second person in that they communicate significantly less of the second person's feelings than the second person has communicated themselves.

Level Two–When the first person responds to the expressed feelings of the second person, he does so in such a way that he subtracts noticeable affect from the communications of the second person.

Level Three–The expressions of the first person in response to the expressed feelings of the second person are essentially interchangeable with those of the second person in that they express essentially the same affect and meaning.

Level Four–The responses of the first person add noticeably to the expressions of the second person in such a way as to express feelings at a level deeper than the second person was able to express himself.

Level Five–The first person's responses add significantly to the feeling and meaning of expressions of the second person in such a way as to (1) accurately express feeling levels below what the person himself was able to express or (2) in the event of ongoing deep self-exploration on the second person's part, to be fully with him in his deepest moments.

APPENDIX C

THE COMMUNICATION OF RESPECT IN
INTERPERSONAL PROCESSES

[Carkuff as presented by C. H. Patterson (1974) pp. 59-60]

Level One–The verbal and behavioral expressions of the first person communicate a clear lack of respect (or negative regard) for the second person.

Level Two–The first person responds to the second person in such a way as to communicate little respect for the feelings, experiences, and potentials of the second person.

Level Three–The first person communicates a positive respect and concern for the second person's feelings, experiences and potentials.

Level Four–The facilitator clearly communicates a very deep respect and concern for the second person.

Level Five–The facilitator communicates the very deepest respect for the second person's worth as a person and his potential as a free individual.

APPENDIX D

FACILITATIVE GENUINENESS IN INTERPERSONAL PROCESSES

[Carkuff as presented by C. H. Patterson (1974) pp. 65-67]

Level One–The first person's verbalizations are clearly unrelated to what he is feeling at the moment, or his only genuine responses are negative in regard to the second person and appear to have a totally destructive effect upon the second person.

Level Two–The first person's verbalizations are slightly unrelated to what he is feeling at the moment, or when his responses are genuine they are negative in regard to the second person; the first person does not appear to know how to employ his negative reactions as a basis for inquiry into the relationship.

Level Three–The first person provides no "negative cues" between what he says and what he feels, but he provides no positive cues to indicate a really genuine response to the second person.

Level Four–The facilitator presents some positive cues indicating a genuine response (whether positive or negative) in a non-destructive manner to the second person.

Level Five–The facilitator is freely and deeply himself in a non-exploitative relationship with the second person.

APPENDIX E

CONCRETENESS OR SPECIFICITY OF EXPRESSION IN INTERPERSONAL PROCESSES

[Carkuff as presented by C. H. Patterson (1974) pp. 69-70]

Level One–The first person leads or allows all discussion with the second person to deal only with vague and anonymous generalities.

Level Two–The first person frequently leads or allows even discussions of material personally relevant to the second person to be dealt with on a vague and abstract level.

Level Three–The first person at times enables the second person to discuss personally relevant material in specific and concrete terminology.

Level Four–The facilitator is frequently helpful in enabling the second person to fully develop in concrete and specific terms almost all instances of concern.

Level Five–The facilitator is always helpful in guiding the discussion, so that the second person may discuss fluently, directly, and completely specific feelings and experiences.

APPENDIX F

RAPPORT EVALUATION FORM

(Sumerall and Oehlert, 1999a)

1 = not at all
2 = minimally, improvement expected
3 = somewhat, acceptable
4 = skill demonstrated at an above average level
5 = superior

1. Trainee demonstrated appropriate type and
    frequency of eye contact.   1 2 3 4 5

2. Trainee demonstrated appropriate body
    language to express interest.   1 2 3 4 5

3. Trainee expressed interest in patient's concerns
    through appropriate questions/statements.   1 2 3 4 5

4. Trainee helped the patient to feel at ease.   1 2 3 4 5

5. Therapist addressed patient's emotional status.   1 2 3 4 5

6. Trainee expressed empathy.   1 2 3 4 5

7. The trainee modified her/his style as appropriate.   1 2 3 4 5

8. Trainee addressed patient's concerns about the
    therapy process.   1 2 3 4 5

9. Trainee encouraged patient to thoroughly
    discuss her/his situation.   1 2 3 4 5

10. Trainee conveyed an appreciation of
    the patient's situation.   1 2 3 4 5

11. Trainee attended to the expressed affect of the patient.   1 2 3 4 5

12. Trainee is aware of the patient's capacity to understand potential causal variables in her/his situation.   1 2 3 4 5

13. Trainee discussed the goal of therapy.   1 2 3 4 5

14. The patient understood the goals of therapy.   1 2 3 4 5

15. Trainee expressed knowledge of the patient's disorder.   1 2 3 4 5

16. Trainee's interactions suggested competence.   1 2 3 4 5

17. The patient recognized the trainee's expertise.   1 2 3 4 5

18. Trainee guided patient to an understanding of their disorder.   1 2 3 4 5

19. Trainee stated therapeutic plans.   1 2 3 4 5

20. Trainee developed an understanding of the patient's view of their situation/disorder.   1 2 3 4 5

APPENDIX G

TECHNIQUES FORM

(Sumerall and Oehlert, 1999b)

Indicate which interview technique produced an effective or ineffective response using the following five point scale:

1 = completely ineffective (e.g., therapist statement shifted response away from therapeutic focus)
2 = minimal impact on therapeutic process (e.g., no new information gathered, response not entirely relevant to advancing therapy)
3 = acceptable impact on therapeutic process (e.g., continued therapy on defined course)
4 = significant response occurred (e.g., patient showed willingness to pursue new possibilities in understanding situation/disorder)
5 = major impact noted (e.g., patient's response suggested new insight)

Closed-ended questions	1 2 3 4 5
Open-ended questions	1 2 3 4 5
Probes	1 2 3 4 5
Interpretations	1 2 3 4 5
Confrontation	1 2 3 4 5
Feedback	1 2 3 4 5
Paraphrasing	1 2 3 4 5
Self-disclosure	1 2 3 4 5
Encouraging	1 2 3 4 5
Information providing	1 2 3 4 5

Instructions	1 2 3 4 5
Direct advice	1 2 3 4 5
Paradoxical instructions	1 2 3 4 5
Cognitive restructuring	1 2 3 4 5
Coaching	1 2 3 4 5
Requests to be more specific	1 2 3 4 5
Reflection of meaning	1 2 3 4 5
Reflection of feeling	1 2 3 4 5
Requests to give reasons for pathology	1 2 3 4 5
Focusing	1 2 3 4 5
Using metaphor	1 2 3 4 5
Request for clarification	1 2 3 4 5
Accenting	1 2 3 4 5
Summarizing	1 2 3 4 5

Above techniques discussed in detail in Benjamin (1981), Hackney and Cormier (1979), Brammer (1979), and Ivey (1988).

APPENDIX H

INTERVENTION COMPETENCY CHECKLIST

(Oehlert, 1999a)

Trainee's Name: _____ Supervisor/Evaluator: _____

Date: _____

Type of Intervention (e.g., cognitive therapy) _____

Mode of Intervention (individual, couple, family, group) _____

Age Classification of Client (infant, child, adolescent, young adult, adult, elderly) _____

1. Articulated understanding of a theory of underlying psychopathology associated with above intervention.

     Yes

     No

2. Defined and explicitly articulated the procedures associated with the psychotherapy system.

     Yes

     No

3. Articulated how the theory of psychopathology is integrally related to its allied psychotherapy system.

     Yes

     No

4. Demonstrated knowledge of the effectiveness of the derived psychotherapeutic techniques.

     Yes

     No

5. Provided verifiable empirical support for the effectiveness of the intervention.

     Yes

     No

6. Demonstrated effectiveness using the selected intervention at the following level:

Individual Therapy

_____ Level One: The trainee is able to effectively work with a client who presents with a single, focal issue (Axis I only). Effectiveness is demonstrated by positive outcome via patient self-report, rapid assessment instruments, and/or behavioral observations.

_____ Level Two: The trainee is able to effectively work with a client with cognitive impairment, dual diagnosis, social/familial impairment or complex psychiatric and behavioral deficits. Effectiveness is demonstrated by movement toward or achievement of treatment goals established early in the therapeutic process.

_____Level Three: The trainee is able to effectively work with a client with a chronic level of psychosis or personality disorders. Effectiveness is demonstrated by evidence of good life adjustment. This level could also be demonstrated by effectively handling an acute suicide intervention or acute psychotic intervention.

Group Therapy

_____ Level One: The trainee participates as a co-facilitator of a group with a senior staff assuming major responsibility for outcome.

_____ Level Two: The trainee serves as leader of a psychoeducational or highly structured group with high functioning clients/patients. Effectiveness is demonstrated by prepost measures assessing improvement in patient functioning or increase in patient knowledge.

_____ Level Three: The trainee leads a therapy process group with a blend of diverse patients. Effectiveness is demonstrated by positive outcome via patient self-report, rapid assessment instruments, and/or behavioral observations.

APPENDIX I

SAMPLE TEST FOR ASSESSMENT OF
BASIC ETHICAL KNOWLEDGE

(Oehlert, 1999b)

1. List (and briefly explain) the Six *General Principles* (APA, 1992) by which psychologists, as members of the American Psychological Association, agree to abide.

A.

B.

C.

D.

E.

F.

2. List (and briefly explain) the Eight categories of *Ethical Standards* (APA, 1992) by which psychologists, as members of the American Psychological Association, agree to abide.

A.

B.

C.

D.

E.

F.

G.

H.

3. Which of the following issues are addressed in the Ethical Principles (1992). Check all that apply.

❏ Offering inducements for research participants

❏ Conflict between ethical principles and the law

❏ Maintaining test security

❏ Computer security

❏ Media presentations

❏ Informed consent to therapy

❏ Confidentiality

❏ Conflictual relationships

❏ Payment sources, plans, settings, and methods

❏ Academic settings, teaching dilemmas and concerns about training

❏ Forensic psychology

❏ Couple and family relationships

❏ Sexual intimacies with former therapy patients

❏ Sexual intimacies with student trainees

❏ Terminating the professional relationship

❏ Pro-bono work

❏ Sexual intimacies with current patients or clients

❏ Permission for electronic recording of interviews

❏ Number of secretaries needed per professional in a group practice

❏ Disclosure of information

❏ Design of education and training programs

❏ Maintaining test security

❏ Accuracy in teaching

❏ Assessing supervisee performance

❏ Sexual harassment

❏ Referral practices

❏ Order in which standardized assessments should be given

❏ Payment for referrals

❏ Soliciting testimonials from clients

❑ Appropriate fee to charge for therapy

❑ Bartering

❑ Avoiding all social and non-professional contacts with clients

❑ Psychologists' personal problems

❑ Misrepresentation of fees

❑ Limits of certainty related to diagnosis, judgments, or predictions about individuals

❑ Using outdated assessments

❑ Social responsibility

❑ Integrity

❑ Respect for people's rights and dignity

❑ Use of collection agencies to collect fees

❑ Releasing raw test results

❑ Use of automated scoring systems

❑ Compensating the local news reporter for mentioning group practice in a news article

❑ How to get informed consent from an incompetent individual

APPENDIX J

SAMPLE TEST FOR BASIC KNOWLEDGE OF ETHICAL DECISION MAKING PROCESSES

(Oehlert, 1999c)

1. Identify Kitchener's (1984)–five fundamental ethical principles.
   a. Benefit others (Beneficience).
   b. Do not harm (Non-maleficence).
   c. Respect others autonomy (Freedom of Choice).
   d. Be just or fair (Justice).
   e. Be faithful (Fidelity).

2. Describe Redlich and Pope (1980) seven-step approach to ethical decision-making.
   a. Above all, do no harm.
   b. Practice only with competence.
   c. Do not exploit.
   d. Treat people with respect for their dignity as human beings.
   e. Protect confidentiality.
   f. Act only with informed consent.
   g. Promote equity and justice.

3. Describe Keith-Spiegel and Koocher (1985) eight-step problem-solving approach.
   a. Describe the parameters of the situation.
   b. Define the potential issues involved.
   c. Consult the guidelines, if any, already available that might apply to the resolution of each issue.
   d. Evaluate the rights, responsibilities, and welfare of all affected parties.
   e. Generate the alternative decision possible for each issue.
   f. Enumerate the consequences of making each decision.
   g. Present any evidence that the various consequences or benefits resulting from each decision will actually occur.
   h. Make the decision.

106

4. Describe Rest's (1983) four components of moral behavior.
   - Moral Sensitivity
   - Moral Reasoning
   - Choosing
   - Executing Choice

APPENDIX K

CHECKLIST FOR ASSESSING ETHICAL
DECISION MAKING

(Oehlert, 1999d)

Based on Rest's (1984) Model

Brief Description of Episode:

Use the following rating scale to answer each statement below:

1----------------------2-------------------------3-----------------------4----------------------5
strongly disagree   disagree   borderline   agree   strongly agree

Moral Sensitivity:

    a. Trainee fully identifies ethical dimensions of the situation.   1 2 3 4 5

    b. Trainee recognizes their actions affect the welfare of another. 1 2 3 4 5

Moral Reasoning:

    c. Trainee differentiates between ethical and unethical choices. 1 2 3 4 5

    d. Trainee consults code of ethics to support decision-making. 1 2 3 4 5

    e. Trainee identifies ethical conflicts–if present. 1 2 3 4 5

Choosing:

    f. Trainee is able to weigh ethical values against other values 1 2 3 4 5
      such as comfort, professional gain, etc.

    g. Trainee is able to use ethical decision-making processes. 1 2 3 4 5

Executing Action:

    h. Trainee is steadfast in doing what is right. 1 2 3 4 5

    i. Trainee demonstrates ego strength in decision-making process. 1 2 3 4 5

    j. Trainee is aware and willing to suffer consequences of acting 1 2 3 4 5
      ethically.

Total Points _____/100
Minimal Standard for Competency ___%

REFERENCES

Alspach, J. G. (1984). Designing a competency-based orientation for critical care nurses. *Heart and Lung, 13*, 655-662.

American Psychological Association. (1983). *Taskforce report on the evaluation of education, training, and service in psychology.* Final report, James Scheimer, Administrative Officer. Washington, DC: Author.

American Psychological Association. (1992). *Ethical principles of psychologists and code of conduct.* Washington, DC: Author.

American Psychological Association Office of Program Consultation and Accreditation. (1996). *Book 1: Guidelines and principles for accreditation of programs in professional psychology.* Washington DC: Author.

Ansell, C., & Ross, H. (1990). Reply to Pope and Bajt. *American Psychologist, 45,* 399.

Association of Psychology Postdoctoral and Internship Centers & American Psychological Association. (1997). *Proceedings from the National Working Conference on Supply and Demand.* Washington, DC: American Psychological Association.

Beck, A. T. (1976). *Cognitive therapy and the emotional disorders.* Madison, WI: International Universities Press, Inc.

Benjamin, A. (1981). *The helping interview* (3rd ed.). Dallas, TX: Houghton Mifflin.

Bent, R. J. (1991). The professional core competency areas. In R. L. Peterson, J. D. McHolland, R. J. Bent, E. Davis-Russell, G. E. Edwall, K. Polite, D. L. Singer, & G. Stricker (Eds.), *The core curriculum in professional psychology* (pp. 77-81). Washington, DC: American Psychological Association.

Bergan, J. R. (1977). *Behavioral consultation.* Columbus, OH: Merrill.

Bergan, J. R., & Tombari, M. L. (1975). The analysis of verbal interactions occurring during consultation. *Journal of School Psychology, 13,* 209-226.

Bernal, M. E., & Castro, F. G. (1994). Are clinical psychologists prepared for services and research with ethnic minorities? *American Psychologist, 49,* 797-805.

Bernard, J. M., & Goodyear, R. K. (1992). *Fundamentals of clinical supervision.* Boston: Allyn & Bacon.

Bersoff, D. (1975). Professional ethics and legal responsibilities: On the horns of a dilemma. *The Journal of School Psychology, 13,* 359-376.

Bersoff, D. N. (Ed.). (1995). *Ethical conflicts in psychology.* Washington, DC: American Psychological Association.

Blakey, W. A., Fantuzzo, J. W., & Moon, G. W. (1985). An automated competency-based model for teaching skills in the administration of the WAIS-R. *Professional Psychology, 16,* 641-647.

109

Brammer, L. M. (1979). *The helping relationship: Process and skills* (2nd ed.). Englewood Cliffs, NJ: Prentice-Hall.

Caplan, G. (1970). *The theory and practice of mental health consultation.* New York: Basic Books.

Carkhuff, R. R. (1969). *Helping and human relations: Volume II, Practice and research.* New York: Holt, Rinehart, & Winston.

Chambers, D. W., & Glassman, P. (1997). A primer on competency based evaluation. *Journal of Dental Education, 61,* 651-666.

Coleman, H. L. K. (1997). Portfolio assessment of multicultural counseling competence. In D. B. Pope-Davis & H. L. K. Coleman (Eds.), *Multicultural counseling competencies: Assessment, education and training, and supervision.* (pp. 43-59). Thousand Oaks, CA: Sage.

Cook, T. D., & Campbell, D. T. (1979). *Quasi-experimentation: Design and analysis issues for field settings.* Boston: Houghton Mifflin.

D'Andrea, M., Daniels, J., & Heck, R. (1991). Evaluating the impact of multicultural counseling training. *Journal of Counseling and Development, 70,* 143-150.

DeCato, C. M. (1992). Development of a method for competency-based training in Rorschach scoring. *The Journal of Training and Practice in Professional Psychology, 6,* 59-66.

Diener, E., & Crandall, R. (1978). *Ethics in social and behavioral research.* Chicago: University of Chicago Press.

Eberlein, L. (1987). Introducing ethics to beginning psychologists: A problem-solving approach. *Professional Psychology: Research and Practice, 18,* 353-359.

Erchul, W. P. (1987). A relational communication analysis of control in school consultation. *Professional School Psychology, 2,* 113-124.

Erchul, W. P., & Chewning, T. G. (1990). Behavioral consultation from a request-centered relational communication perspective. *School Psychology Quarterly, 5,* 1-20.

Fantuzzo, J. W. (1984, Winter). Mastery: A competency-based training model for clinical psychologists. *The Clinical Psychologist,* 29-30.

Fantuzzo, J. W., & Moon, G. W. (1984). Competency mandate: A model for teaching skills in the administration of the WAIS-R. *Journal of Clinical Psychology, 40,* 1053-1059.

Fantuzzo, J. W., Sisemore, T. A., & Spradlin, W. H. (1983). A competency-based model for teaching skills in the administration of intelligence tests. *Professional Psychology: Research and Practice, 14,* 224-231.

Fordyce, W. E., & Meier, M. J. (1987). Respecialization and continuing education. In G. C. Stone, S. M. Weiss, J. D. Matarazzo, N. E. Miller, J. Rodin, C. D. Belar, M. J. Follick, & J. E. Singer (Eds.). *Health psychology: A discipline and a profession.* Chicago: University of Chicago Press.

Fox, R., & Barclay, A. G. (1989). Let a thousand flowers bloom: Or, weed the garden? *American Psychologist, 44,* 55-59.

Frank, J. (1961). *Persuasion and healing.* Baltimore: Johns Hopkins Press.

Galanti, G. (1991). *Caring for patients from different cultures: Case studies from American hospitals.* Philadelphia: University of Pennsylvania Press.

Garfield, S. L., & Kurtz, R. M. (1973). Attitudes toward testing. A survey of directors of internship training. *Journal of Consulting and Clinical Psychology, 40,* 350-355.

Gelso, C. J., Mallinckrodt, B., & Judge, A. B. (1996). Research training environment, attitudes towards research, and research self-efficacy: The revised Research Training Environment Scale. *The Counseling Psychologist, 24,* 304 322.

Greenhalgh, T., & Macfarlane, F. (1997). Towards a competency grid for evidence-based practice. *Journal of Evaluation in Clinical Practice, 3,* 161-165.

Greenwood, L. F., Lewis, D. W., & Burgess, R. C. (1998). How competent do our graduates feel? *Journal of Dental Education, 62,* 307-313.

Hackney, H., & Cormier, L. S. (1979). *Counseling strategies and objectives* (2nd ed.). Englewood Cliffs, NJ: Prentice-Hall.

Handlesman, M. M. (1986). Problems with ethics training by "osmosis." *Professional Psychology: Research and Practice, 17,* 371-372.

Helms, J. E., & Richardson, T. Q. (1997). How "Multiculturalism" obscures race and culture as differential aspects of counseling competency. In D. B. Pope-Davis & H. L. K. Coleman (Eds.), *Multicultural counseling competencies: Assessment, education and training, and supervision.* (pp. 60-79). Thousand Oaks, CA: Sage.

Hill, D., Stalley, P., Pennington, D., Besser, M., & McCarthy, W. (1997). Competency-based learning in traumatology. *The American Journal of Surgery, 173,* 136-140.

Hogan, R. A. (1964). Issues and approaches in supervision. *Psychotherapy: Theory, research, and practice, 1,* 139-141.

Hunt, D. E. (1971). *Matching models in education. The coordination of teaching methods with student characteristics.* Toronto: OntarioInstitute for Studies in Education.

Hyland, T. (1993). Competence, knowledge, and education. *Journal of Philosophy of Education, 27,* 57-68.

Illback, R. J., Maher, C. A., & Kopplin, D. (1991). Consultation and education competency. In R. L. Peterson, J. D. McHolland, R. J. Bent, E. Davis Russell, G. E. Edwall, K. Polite, D. L. Singer, & G. Stricker (Eds.). *The core curriculum in professional psychology* (pp. 115-120). Washington, DC: American Psychological Association.

Ivey, A. E. (1988). *Intentional interviewing and counseling: Facilitating client development* (2nd ed.). Pacific Grove, CA: Brooks/Cole.

Johnson, H. H., & Solso, R. L. (1978). *An introduction to experimental design in psychology: A case approach.* New York: Harper & Row, Publisher, Inc.

Jordan, A. E., & Meara, N. M. (1990). Ethics and the professional practice of psychologists. *Professional Psychology: Research and Practice, 21,* 107-114.

Kahn, J. H., & Gelso, C. J. (1997). Factor structure of the Research Training Environment Scale-Revised: Implications for research training in applied psychology. *The Counseling Psychologist, 25,* 22-37.

Kaufman, R. A. (1971). A possible integrative model for the systematic and durable improvement of education. *American Psychologist, 26,* 250-257.

Keith-Spiegel, P., & Koocher, G. P. (1985). *Ethics in psychology: Professional standards and cases.* Hillsdale, NJ: Erlbaum.

Kitchener, K. (1986). Teaching applied ethics in counselor education: An integration of psychological processes and philosophical analysis. *Journal of Counseling and Development, 64,* 306-310.

Kitchener, K. S. (1984). Intuition, critical evaluation, and ethical principles: The foundation for ethical decisions in counseling psychology. *The Counseling Psychologist, 12,* 43-56.

Knight, B. (1992). *Older adults in psychotherapy: Case histories.* Newbury Park, CA: Sage.

Knight, B. Santos, J., Teri, L., & Lawton, M. P. (1995). Introduction: The development of training in clinical geropsychology. In B. G. Knight, L. Teri, P. Wohlford, & J. Santos (Eds.). *Mental health services for older adults: Implications for training and practice in geropsychology* (pp. 1-8). Washington, DC: American Psychological Association.

Kratochwill, T. R. (1982). School psychology: Dimensions of its dilemmas and future directions. *Professional Psychology, 13,* 977-989.

Kratochwill, T. R., & Bergan, J. R. (1978). Training school psychologists: Some perspectives on a competency-based behavioral consultation model. *Professional Psychology, 9,* 71-82.

Kratochwill, T. R., & Bergan, J. R. (1990). *Behavioral consultation in applied settings: An individual guide.* New York: Plenum Press.

Kratochwill, T. R., Elliott, S. N., & Busse, R. T. (1995). Behavior consultation: A five-year evaluation of consultant and client outcomes. *School Psychology Quarterly, 10,* 87-117.

Kratochwill, T. R., Sheridan, S. M., Rotto, P. & Salmon, D. (1991). Preparation of school psychologists in consultation service delivery: Practical, theoretical, and research considerations. In T. R. Kratchowill, S. N. Elliott, & M. Gettinger (Eds.), *Advances in school psychology* (Vol. VIII, pp. 115-152). Hillsdale, NJ: Erlbaum Associates.

Kratochwill, T. R., & VanSomeren, K. R. (1984). Training behavioral consultants: Issues and directions. *The Behavior Therapist, 7,* 19-22.

Kratochwill, T. R., VanSomeren, K. R., & Sheridan, S. M. (1989). Training behavioral consultants: A competency-based model to teach interview skills. *Professional School Psychology, 4,* 41-58.

Krieshok, T. S., Somberg, D., & Cantrell, P. J. (1996, August). *Dissertation while on internship: Obstacles and predictors of progress.* Poster presented at the 104th Annual Convention of the American Psychological Association, Toronto, Ontario, Canada.

LaFramboise, T. D., Coleman, H. L. K., & Hernandez, A. (1991). Development and factor structure of the Cross-Cultural Counseling Inventory Revised. *Professional Psychology: Research and Practice, 22,* 380-388.

Logsdon, R. G. (1995). Psychopathology and treatment: Curriculum and research needs. In B. G. Knight, L. Teri, P. Wohlford, & J. Santos (Eds.), *Mental health services for older adults: Implications for training and practice in geropsychology* (pp. 41-51). Washington, DC: American Psychological Association.

Lopez, S. J. (1996). *Cultural Sensitivity Self-Report.* Unpublished measure. University of Kansas.

Lopez, S. J., Oehlert, M. E., & Moberly, R. L. (1996). Selection criteria for APA-accredited internship programs: A survey of training directors. *Professional Psychology: Research and Practice, 27,* 518-520.

Lykes, M. B., & Hellstedt, J. C. (1987). Field training in community social psychology: A competency-based, self-directed learning model. *Journal of Community Psychology, 15*, 417-428.

Madsen, C. K., & Alley, J. M. (1979). The effect of reinforcement on attentiveness: A comparison of behaviorally trained music therapists and other professionals with implications for competency-based academic preparation. *Journal of Music Therapy, 16*, 70-82.

Martens, B. K., Witt, J. C., Elliott, S. N., & Darveaux, D. X. (1985). Teacher judgments concerning the acceptability of school-based interventions. *Professional Psychology: Research and Practice, 16*, 191-198.

McCann, A. L., Babler, W. J., & Cohen, P. A. (1998). Lessons learned from the competency-based curriculum initiative at Baylor College of Dentistry. *Journal of Dental Education, 62*, 197-207.

Meara, N. M., Schmidt, L. D., & Day, J. D. (1996). Principles and virtues: A foundation for ethical decisions, policies, and character. *The Counseling Psychologist, 24*, 4-77.

Miles, M. B., & Huberman, A. M. (1984). *Qualitative data analysis: A sourcebook of new methods.* Beverly Hills, CA: Sage Publications.

Mish, F. C. (Ed.). (1985). *Webster's Ninth New Collegiate Dictionary.* Springfield, MA: Merriam-Webster, Inc.

Mishler, E. G. (1986). *Research interviewing: Context and narrative.* Cambridge, MA: Harvard University Press.

Mitrani, A., Dalziel, M., & Fitt. D. (1992). *Competency based human resource management.* Kogan Page: London, England.

Moon, G. W., Fantuzzo, J. W., & Gorsuch, R. L. (1986). Teaching WAIS-R administration skills: Comparison of MASTERY model to other existing clinical training modalities. *Professional Psychology: Research and Practice, 17*, 31-35.

Mowder, B. A. (1979). Training school psychologists: The issue of competency-based education. *Professional Psychology, 10*, 697-702.

Musgrove, W. J. (1974). A scale to measure attitudes toward behavior modification. *Psychology in the Schools, 11*, 392-396.

O'Brien, K. M., & Lucas, M. S. (1993). *The Research Attitudes Measure.* (Available from K. M. O'Brien, Psychology Department, University of Maryland, College Park, MD 20742).

O'Dell, S. L., Tarler-Benlolo, L., & Flynn, J. M. (1979). An instrument to measure knowledge of behavioral principles as applied to children. *Journal of Behavior Therapy and Experimental Psychiatry, 10*, 29-34.

Oehlert, M. E. (1999a). *Intervention Competency Checklist.* Unpublished instrument.

Oehlert, M. E. (1999b). *Sample Test for Assessment of Basic Ethical Knowledge.* Unpublished instrument.

Oehlert, M. E. (1999c). *Sample Test for Basic Knowledge of Ethical Decision Making Processes.* Unpublished instrument.

Oehlert, M. E. (1999d). *Checklist for Assessing Ethical Decision Making.* Unpublished instrument.

Oehlert, M. E., Sumerall, S. W., & Lopez, S. J. (1998). *Internship selection in professional psychology: A comprehensive guide for students, faculty, and training directors.* Springfield, IL: Charles C Thomas.

Othmer, E., & Othmer, S. C. (1994). *The clinical interview using DSM IV, Volume I: Fundamentals.* Washington, DC: American Psychiatric Press.

Patterson, C. H. (1974). *Relationship counseling and psychotherapy.* New York: Harper & Row.

Pelsma, D. M., & Borgers, S. B. (1986). Experience-based ethics: A development model of learning ethical reasoning. *Journal of Counseling and Development, 64,* 311-314.

Peterson, R. L., McHolland, J. D., Bent, R. J., Davis-Russell, E., Edwall, G. E., Polite, K., Singer, D. L., & Stricker. G. (Eds.), (1991). *The core curriculum in professional psychology.* Washington, DC: American Psychological Association.

Pfeiffer, S. I. (1981). A school psychology program's initial evaluation of its competency-based training model. *Psychology in the Schools, 18,* 60-66.

Polite, K., & Bourg, E. (1991). Relationship competency. In R. L. Peterson, J. D. McHolland, R. J. Bent, E. Davis-Russell, G. E. Edwall, K. Polite, D. L. Singer, & G. Stricker (Eds.), *The core curriculum in professional Psychology* (pp. 83-88). Washington, DC: American Psychological Association.

Ponterotto, J. G. (1997). Multicultural counseling training: A competency model and national survey. In D. B. Pope-Davis & H. L. K. Coleman (Eds.), *Multicultural counseling competencies: Assessment, education and training, and supervision.* (pp. 111 -130). Thousand Oaks, CA: Sage.

Ponterotto, J. G., Sanchez, C. M., & Magids, D. M. (1991, August). *Initial development and validation of the Multicultural Counseling Awareness Scale.* Paper presented at the 99th Annual Convention of the American Psychological Association, San Francisco, CA.

Pope, K., & Bajt, T. (1988). When laws and values conflict: A dilemma for psychologists. *American Psychologist, 43,* 828-829.

Proctor, J. (1991). *Using competences for management development.* Henley Distance Learning Limited for NHS Training Directorate, HMSO: London, England.

Redlich, R. C., & Pope, K. S. (1980). Ethics of mental health training. *Journal of Nervous and Mental Disease, 168,* 709-714.

Reilly, D. H., Barclay, J., & Culbertson, F. (1977). The current status of competency-based training, Part 1: Validity, reliability, logistical, and ethical issues. *Journal of School Psychology, 15,* 68-74.

Rest, J. R. (1983). Morality. In J. Flavel & E. Markham (Eds.), Cognitive development, Volume IV. P. Mussen (General Ed.). *Manual of child psychology* (pp. 520-629). New York: Wiley.

Rest, J. R. (1984). Research on moral development: Implications for training counseling psychologists. *The Counseling Psychologist, 12,* 19-29.

Ridley, C. R. (1995). *Overcoming unintentional racism in counseling and therapy: A practitioner's guide to intentional intervention.* Thousand Oaks, CA: Sage.

Ridley, C. R., Espelage, D. L., & Rubinstein, K. J. (1997). Course development in multicultural counseling. In D. B. Pope-Davis & H. L. K. Coleman (Eds.), *Multicultural counseling competencies: Assessment, education and training, and supervision.* (pp. 131 -158). Thousand Oaks, CA: Sage.

Ridley, C. R., Mendoza, D. W., Kanitz, B. E., Angermeier, L., & Zenk, R. (1994). Cultural sensitivity in multicultural counseling: A perceptual schema model. *Journal of Counseling Psychology, 41,* 125-136.

Rogers, C. R. (1957). The necessary and sufficient conditions of therapeutic personality change. *Journal of Consulting Psychology, 21,* 95-103.

Ryan, J. J., Weaver, T., & Lopez, S. J. (1999). *Administration checklist for the Wechsler Memory Scale-III.* Unpublished measure.

Sambandan, S. (1995). Competence and performance are measurable but do not equate with practice (letter). *British Medical Journal, 311,* 393.

Sattler, J. M., & Ryan, J. J. (1999). *Assessment of children: Revised and updated third edition, WAIS-III supplement.* San Diego: Jerome M. Sattler, Publisher, Inc.

Schlomer, R. S., Anderson, M. A., & Shaw, R. (1997). Teaching strategies and knowledge retention. *Journal of Nursing Staff Development, 13,* 249-253.

Scott, K. J., Ingram, K. M., Vitanza, S. A., Smith, N. G. (1998). *Training in supervision: A survey of current practices.* Poster session presented at the annual convention of the American Psychological Association in San Francisco, CA.

Shakow, D. (1947). Recommended graduate training programs in clinical psychology. *American Psychologist, 2,* 539-558.

Sheridan, S. M. (1992). Consultant and client outcomes of competence based behavioral consultation training. *School Psychology Quarterly, 1,* 245 270.

Sheridan, S. M., Salmon, D., Kratchowill, T. R., & Rotto, P. J. (1992). Conceptual and practical considerations for behavioral consultation training. *Journal of Educational and Psychological Consultation, 3,* 193-218.

Slate, J. R., & Jones, C. H. (1990). Student error in administering the WISC-R: Identify problem areas. *Measurement and Evaluation in Counseling and Development, 23,* 137-140.

Slate, J. R., Jones, C. H., Coutler, C., & Covert, T. L. (1992). Practitioners' administration and scoring of the WISC-R: Evidence that we do err. *Journal of School Psychology, 30,* 77-82.

Slate, J. R., Jones, C. J., & Murray, R. A. (1991). Teaching, administration, and scoring of the WAIS-R: An empirical evaluation of practice administrations. *Professional Psychology: Research & Practice, 22,* 375-379.

Slate, J. R., Jones, C. H., Murray, R. A., & Coutler, C. (1993). Evidence that practitioners err in administering and scoring the WAIS-R. *Measurement and Evaluation in Counseling and Development, 25,* 156-161.

Smith, S. R., & Fuller, B. (1996). MD2000: A competency-based curriculum for the Brown University School of Medicine. *Medicine and Health, 79,* 292-298.

Smyer, M. A., & Downs, M. G. (1995). Psychopharmacology: An essential element in educating clinical psychologists for working with older adults. In B. G. Knight, L. Teri, P. Wohlford, & J. Santos (Eds.), *Mental health services for older adults: Implications for training and practice in geropsychology* (pp. 73-83). Washington, DC: American Psychological Association.

Sodowsky, G. R., Taffe, R. C., Gutkin, T. B., & Wise, S. L. (1994). Development of the Multicultural Counseling Inventory: A self-report measure of multicultural competencies. *Journal of Counseling and Development, 41,* 137 148.

Sodowsky, G. R., Kuo-Jackson, P. Y., & Loya, G. J. (1997). Outcome of training in the philosophy of assessment. In D. B. Pope-Davis & H. L. K. Coleman (Eds.), *Multicultural counseling competencies: Assessment, education and training, and supervision* (pp. 3-42). Thousand Oaks, CA: Sage.

Spruill, J., Kohout, J., & Gehlmann, S. (1997). *Final Report of the American Psychological Association Working Group on the Implications of Changes in the Health Care Delivery System for the Education, Training and Continuing Professional Education of Psychologists.* Washington DC: American Psychological Association.

Stoltenberg, C. (1981). Approaching supervision from a developmental perspective: The counselor complexity model. *Journal of Counseling Psychology, 28*, 59-65.

Stratford, R. (1994). A competency approach to educational psychology practice: The implications for quality. *Educational and Child Psychology, 11*, 21-28.

Sumerall, S. W., & Oehlert, M. E. (1999a). *Rapport Evaluation Form.* Unpublished instrument.

Sumerall, S. W., & Oehlert, M. E. (1999b). *Techniques Form.* Unpublished instrument.

Task Force on Promotion and Dissemination of Psychological Procedures. (1993). *A report adopted by Division 12 Board,* 1-17.

Teague, L. (1983). An examination of communication patterns results from a conjoint parent/child sex education program. *Masters Abstracts International, 21*, 317.

Trierweiler, S. J., & Stricker, G. (1991). Research and evaluation competency: Training the local clinical scientist. In R. L. Peterson, J. D. McHolland, R. J. Bent, E. Davis-Russell, G. E. Edwall, K. Polite, D. L. Singer, & G. Stricker (Eds.), *The core curriculum in professional psychology* (pp. 103 113). Washington, DC: American Psychological Association.

Truax, C., & Carkhuff, R. (1964). The old and the new: Theory and research in counseling and psychotherapy. *Personnel and Guidance Journal, 42*, 860-866.

Truax, C. B., & Carkhuff, R. R. (1967). *Toward effective counseling and psychotherapy: Training and Practice.* Chicago, IL: Aldine.

U. S. Department of Commerce. (1989). *United States Department of Commerce: Bureau of Census statistical abstract of the United States for 1989.* Washington, DC: Author.

Vasquez, M. J. (1992). Psychologist as clinical supervisor: Promoting ethical practices. *Professional Psychology: Research and Practice, 23*, 196-202.

Wampold, B. E., & Holloway, E. L. (1997). Methodology, design, and evaluation, in psychotherapy supervision research. In C. E. Watkins (Ed.). *Handbook of Psychotherapy Supervision* (pp. 11-27). New York: John Wiley & Sons.

Watkins, C. E. (1998). Psychotherapy supervision in the 21st century: Some pressing needs and impressing possibilities. *Journal of Psychotherapy Research and Practice, 7*, 93-101.

Whitten, J., Slate, J. R., Jones, C. H., Shine, A. E., & Raggio, D. (1994). Examiner errors in administering and scoring the WPPSI-R. *Journal of Psychoeducational Assessment, 12*, 49-54.

Wolber, G. J., & Carne, W. F. (1993). *Writing psychological reports: A guide for clinicians.* Sarasoata, FL: Professional Resource Press.

Woodruffe, C. (1991, September). Competent by any other name. *Personnel Management,* 30-33.

INDEX